Global education 'reform'
building resistance and solidarity

edited by Gawain Little

First published in 2015 by Manifesto Press

© Gawain Little *editor* and individual authors
All rights reserved

ISBN 978-1-907464-12-6
The moral rights of the authors have been asserted

Typset in Bodoni and Gill
Printed in Britain by Russell Press

Contents

Foreword Education is a public good *Christine Blower*

Preface Building a movement to win *Angelo Gavrielatos*

Editor's Introduction *Gawain Little*

1. What teachers need to know about the 'Global Education Reform Movement' *Susan Robertson*

2. The impact of the USA and UK on public education in Australia *Maurie Mulheron*

3. Teacher solidarity across borders: an essential response to neoliberal globalisation *Larry Kuehn*

4. Lessons from the Global South *Lars Dahlström & Brook Lemma*

5. Neoliberal capitalism dismantling public education in India *Ravi Kumar*

   Interlude: Pearson's new clothes: a modern fairy tale *Teacher Solidarity*

6. Modernising education reforms & government policies against teachers in Ecuador *Edgar Isch L*

7. Venezuela: education for the people *Francisco Dominguez*

8. The unexpected crop: social insurgency and new alternatives for education in Mexico *Hugo Aboites*

9. From resistance to renewal: the emergence of social movement unionism in England *Howard Stevenson & Gawain Little*

10. A city transformed: lessons from the struggle of Chicago teachers *Carol Caref*

11. Reimagining and remaking education: remarks to the NUT–Teacher Solidarity conference *Lois Weiner*

Afterword We are the penicillin to the GERM *Kristine Mayle*

Acknowledgements

This book grew out of a conference jointly organised by the National Union of Teachers (www.teachers.org.uk) and the Teacher Solidarity Research Collaborative (www.teachersolidarity.com) in May 2014. With two exceptions, the 11 chapters are based on presentations given by the authors at this conference. The two additions are Maurie Mulheron's contribution on the Australian education system and the piece by myself and Howard Stevenson on the English education system, both of which have been added specifically for this collection.

I want to thank all the authors who contributed both to this book and to the conference it grew out of. It has been a pleasure and a privilege to read and edit your papers. The conference would never have taken place were it not for Mary Compton, founder and editor of the Teacher Solidarity website. She was both the instigator and driving force throughout. Thanks also to Howard Stevenson; Samidha Garg; David Wilson; Dave Harvey; Kevin Courtney; Phil Katz; Ben Chacko and the staff of the Morning Star; Steph Gilroy-Lowe; Brendan Lee; Nick Wright at Manifesto Press; and Catherine Little.

A special mention for Rosa & Clara Little, who remind me every day how important it is to fight for education and for our children's future.

Finally, I want to thank the teachers whose stories are told within these pages, teachers risking their careers, their liberty and sometimes even their lives because of their belief in the transformative power of education; teachers struggling across the world for a better future for our children.

It is to them that this book is dedicated – A luta continua!

Foreword Education is a Public Good
Christine Blower *General Secretary National Union of Teachers*

EDUCATION IS A human and civil right and a public good. This is a principle on which the National Union of Teachers (NUT) and Education International (EI) stand. It is also enshrined in the constitution of Finland. We stand with the UN rapporteur, Kishore Singh when he says that "states should put an end to market driven education reforms".

The Global Education Reform Movement, characterised by standardised testing, performance-related pay, competition and privatisation, is the very antithesis of education as a public good.

The genesis of GERM can be found in the axis, some would say of evil, between Margaret Thatcher and Ronald Regan. In this publication, Maurie Mulheron traces this in detail, to show how, from the 80s both the US and UK became infected and affected by GERM long before Pasi Sahlberg gave us the expression. The characteristics of GERM, which has blighted our education systems ever since as it spread from country to country, are explored in depth in Susan Robertson's paper.

It was a deep seated concern about the malign influence of GERM on our education systems, our unions and teachers globally that gave rise to a conference in May 2014. The NUT brought together speakers from Venezuela, Mexico, Sweden, Ecuador, British Colombia, the USA and India amongst others to provide insights into the very real effects of GERM and the neo liberal agenda from which it flows.

Since May 2014, as result of work by EI affiliates, a major campaign has been launched at global level. EI is now at the forefront of an anti-GERM anti-privatisation campaign which will seeks to challenge directly the edubisinesses that profit from our children. This campaign will be further deepened and strengthened when EI meets for its World Congress in Summer 2015.

A key focus of this campaign will be Pearson and other privatising edubusinesses. The NUT and AFT have already organised high profile campaigning activities, such as the lobby of the Pearson AGM, with more to follow. The NUT is rightly proud of our Stand up for Education campaign which has sought to engage parents, students and the wider school and education community in the struggle for an education system which is free, fair and inclusive in the UK.

In the NUT we stand ready to play a full part in the campaign to roll back so called low-fee private schools in the global south where aid budgets from the global north are being plundered by the privateers to increase their profit and simultaneously killing off any state-provided school systems.

Despite the day to day pressures that NUT members and teachers in general face, when the realisation dawns that it is the Global Education Reform Movement which is reaching down into their classrooms - causing the workload, curriculum distortion, excessive testing, over-zealous inspection, league table and performance related pay that does so much to damage education - they feel the need to get involved.

This publication, along with the EI campaign and the NUT Stand up for Education campaign provide the arguments to arm teachers and our allies in the fight against GERM. I commend it to you.

Christine Blower

Preface
Angelo Gavrielatos

AS A STUDENT, from the earliest recollections I have of the development of my political consciousness, I recognised the injustice of exploitation of the many by some in positions of relative privilege.

With the guidance of some of my teachers I became determined to act against such injustice and contribute in some small way to ensure that everyone regardless of their background would be able to live a life full of dignity, contributing to society in accordance to their ability and being rewarded in accordance to their need.

I became determined to contribute to the achievement of social justice and peace for all.It is what led me to becoming a teacher unionist and eventually a leader of my union.Becoming a teacher and teacher unionist became my pride and my passion.

That is largely due to the fact that I consider quality education for all and a fair system of industrial relations two key pillars in the achievement of a decent society.I became driven by the fundamental belief in the transformative power of education and what it means to each individual child and the global village in which we live.

A public school, free, secular and universally accessible in every community which would set the standard for high quality education – after all, equity in the provision of education could only be achieved if public schools set that standard.

Of course that meant that public schools would need to be appropriately resourced to deliver with qualified teachers in every classroom a rigorous, rich and rewarding curriculum – to provide every child with the opportunity to achieve his/ her full potential.Unfortunately, this ideal is under greater threat today than it has ever been.The greatest threat to high quality education for all, is the continuing commercialisation and privatisation of education.The market now seems to dominate all aspects of life with boundaries between public and private breaking down.

Around the globe there is an accelerating use of market mechanisms to drive social policy.Schooling which once appeared to be one area that may have been immune from this, is now under considerable threat. The Global 'Education Reform' Movement (GERM) is now largely controlled by the corporate world with deep connections to conservative politicians.

We are now seeing across the world the growth in 'edu-businesses' that have enormous power and influence.

We are already seeing the effects of this agenda with the break-up of traditional school systems such as the growth in Charter Schools in the US, the Free Schools in Sweden, Academies in the UK and more recently Charter Schools in New Zealand.

Worse still, we are seeing the emergence and spread of 'for-profit' schools.Advocates of privatisation argue that applying the free-market principles of choice and competition to the running of schools will drive standards up across the system. The argument goes something like this: removing schools from state control and transferring public funds to private organisations to run them will see their results improve and compel state schools to work harder to keep up with them.However this is demonstrably not true.

Even the OECD warns against applying market mechanisms to the provision of schooling arguing that it leads to a growing segregation of students which has a negative impact on educational outcomes.We are at a pivotal time for the future of education.

We must not let quality public education slip away as a top priority for governments.

It is our job to keep pressing the core message that without properly resourced high quality education for all, society itself will be fundamentally damaged.

We must create a new narrative articulating again why public education has such an important role in each of our societies and why it cannot be outsourced to the private sector. We must make it clear to our political leaders that the commercialisation and privatisation of education are not the answer. It is truly alarming to hear people at the World Bank claiming that low fee, for profit education will help poor countries achieve their Education For All targets.

Are they really suggesting that charging fees will increase access and opportunity for all? Are they really suggesting that the poor must choose between feeding their children, giving them medication or sending them to school? However, we can't do it alone.

The global political landscape requires us to engage in a new deeper strategic analysis of what needs to be done if we are to resist and more importantly reverse current trends. We are dealing with global players the size and reach of which we could not have foreseen some years ago.

And, we, the teacher union movement are in their sights.

This is because we remain the last barrier, the last obstacle between global capital and its desired unfettered access to the limitless, sustainable resource of children and their education.In recognition of this reality we need to commit to a new style of unionism – social movement unionism.

First and foremost, we need to get our house in order.

We must build teacher union unity, membership density and therefore strength.

We also need to reach out and build community alliances in a way we have never done so before.

We need to build alliances with parents and the broader community.

There is no more natural alliance than the one that can and should exist between parents and teachers.

After all, after parents, it is teachers who have the greatest interest in the well-being of children.But of course we need to reach further and deeper than that.

We need to build closer alliances with the broader union movement given that all workers are feeling the negative impact of global capital and its desire to redefine and reduce employment standards and conditions, and of course we need to build alliance with other social movements that share our broad objectives.We need a new style of - doing business".

More of the same will not deliver us success.

We need to make some hard decisions.We can continue to organise campaigns to protest, or we can build a movement to protest and win!

Editor's introduction
Gawain Little

"THERE IS NO ALTERNATIVE" This phrase, famously used by neoliberal British Prime Minister Margaret Thatcher and recently wheeled out by her successor David Cameron, sums up the nature of hegemony – the process by which the rich and powerful establish the social, political and economic norms of society. This is no more evident than in the construction of education policy.

For almost 40 years a dominant narrative has gripped both policy-makers and populations across the world. It asserts that only a competitive, market approach to education, with the attendant standardisation and testing regime, can guarantee high-quality education and that private companies are the only way to deliver it.

This is the GERM. It infects education systems globally and has changed the very nature of education, including restructuring teachers' work and, crucially, children's learning. It threatens to strip away the emancipatory process of education and replace it with a narrow economic process which simply seeks (in the words of its advocates) to add value to human capital.

However, in spite of the overwhelming support of powerful vested interests from national governments to international institutions like the World Bank, IMF and EU, the GERM faces resistance wherever it seeks to embed itself.

Teachers and parents are at the forefront of that resistance. Their fight takes different forms in different countries but, regardless of this, it is the same struggle. In view of this, international solidarity is crucial. This book is intended as a contribution to the practical solidarity which sustains the struggle.

It is written with teachers and teacher union activists in mind but I hope that the stories it tells will also prove useful to parents, researchers, community activists and others concerned about the future of education. Above all, it is intended to be a practical book. By sharing our understanding, our successes and our setbacks, we can strengthen the struggle against a system that would enslave our children to a neoliberal agenda.

In the opening chapter, Susan Robertson sets out the key aspects of the GERM and the threat these pose to our education systems. Her paper looks at how GERM undermines the very elements that support effective learning and identifies the forces that push this agenda regardless.

This understanding of GERM policies and how they reinforce each other is crucial for teachers as it means the difference between being victims of seemingly illogical policies and initiatives and being able to challenge the vision of education and the vested interests from which these policies flow. It also demonstrates the global scale of the attack on education.

This international theme is followed in chapter two as Maurie Mulheron outlines the negative impact that UK and US education have had on the Australian system. The export of regressive policies is an essential feature of the GERM and Maurie's contribution will prove relevant and enlightening for teacher union activists both in the UK, US and Australia, and elsewhere.

Running throughout Maurie's contribution is the process by which the rich and powerful have captured the discourse around education, using a combination of fear and populist reaction to redefine what constitutes 'common sense' in education. This process is revisited in several of the later chapters.

The next three chapters continue to explore the global nature of the GERM. In chapter three, Larry Kuehn addresses the importance of international solidarity in fighting back against the GERM.

Larry's paper draws attention to three main features of GERM – testing, technology and corporate capitalism – he also talks about how the last of these is strengthened through free trade agreements which are "designed to privilege corporate interests by making all aspects of human activity into tradable commodities and limiting the ability of the state to adopt laws or policies that limit the ability of corporations to make profits."

The Transatlantic Trade and Investment Partnership (TTIP) and the Comprehensive Economic and Trade Agreement (CETA) are two such agreements currently being negotiated by the European Union with the USA and Canada respectively. If agreed, these will dramatically increase the powers of corporate capital over education.

In chapter four, Lars Dahlström and Brook Lemma consider, in their study of four African countries, the way in which GERM infects even progressive governments through the involvement of agencies such as the World Bank and IMF. This is a salutary lesson about the power of an international system and the need to develop effective links between our national resistance movements on every level.

Chapter five analyses the link between free market liberalism and conservative ideologies in India, and critiques the role of trade unions and the political left in responding to this agenda. In particular, it refers to the need to challenge teachers' perceptions of themselves as educators and as workers.

We then take a brief interlude to explore the world of Pearson's New Clothes. Pearson is one of the largest global edubusinesses and its role extends from publishing of textbooks, testing materials and data analysis in the Global North to the provision of low-cost for-profit education in the Global South. Challenging GERM and its impact on our children means challenging companies like Pearson and exposing their business operations.

The next three chapters take us to the Americas. In chapter six, Edgar Isch gives his analysis of the failure of the Correa government in Ecuador to establish a truly GERM-free environment, whilst recognising the contradiction between this and the government's investment in education and the progressive moves made, especially in its first term of office.

This links to the analysis presented in chapter four by Lars Dhalstrom and Brook Lemma and opens up a genuine question for teacher union activists: how can we best support the advances made by progressive governments whilst ensuring that we balance the pressure they will inevitably feel from neoliberal institutions and big business with a similar level of 'people pressure'. How can we ensure the correct balance between constructive criticism and undermining left governments?

Chapter seven is unique in this collection in elaborating what happens when a people's government totally rejects neoliberalism and resolves to develop education in the interests of the vast majority of the population. Francisco Dominguez analyses the progress made by the Venezuelan government in spite of the external pressure it feels, not least from its northern neighbour the USA.

Of particular interest here is the way in which the Venezuelan government has managed to combine the development of technology in education with respect for, and the development of, indigenous cultures, rather than the same technology acting as a tool for crude 'westernisation'. This stands in sharp contrast to the examples cited by Larry Kuehn in chapter three and shows that the power of technology can be harnessed for progressive advance where the political will exists.

As Francisco points out, none of this would be possible if the Venezuelan government had not established an economic basis for the development of education by wresting control of the country's oil reserves from the hands of foreign firms and domestic capital. Of course, Venezuela is not the only government to have prioritised progressive educational advance as part of a pro-people platform. Nearby Cuba has regularly been cited as an inspiration by Venezuelan leaders and, as Francisco's paper points out, the Venezuelan approach to eradicating literacy is directly modelled on Cuba's success.

Cuba's astounding model of education, developed and led by the Cuban people themselves, is documented in The Education Revolution by Theodore H. MacDonald (also published by Manifesto) and provides inspiration across Latin America and worldwide. For a small country which has faced five decades of economic blockade by the world's most powerful country to have developed such a strong and progressive education system shows quite what is possible when governments are controlled by the people and not the other way around.

The next three papers strike a similarly optimistic tone, but in very different conditions.

In chapter eight, Hugo Aboites charts the resistance of Mexican teachers to the brutal assaults they have faced from Mexican governments for several decades. This situation is drawn into sharp focus by the disappearance of 43 student teachers on September 26th 2014 following a confrontation with police on the way to a protest.

However, in the face of dire circumstances, Hugo draws attention to the gains that have been achieved in terms of awakening the consciousness of teachers and how this has translated into action to take back control of the education process. It is this process of consciousness-raising which is fundamental to challenging the hegemony of GERM and winning an alternative. This is a process that can only take place through direct involvement in the struggle.

By engaging in resistance and challenging the GERM, we begin to develop an understanding and analysis of both the impact that neoliberalism has on our education systems and what an alternative vision may look like. By sharing our experiences of the struggle, reflecting and learning from each other, we deepen that understanding and that analysis.

The next two chapters bring us back to the UK and US, where the seeds of the GERM were planted.

Chapter nine follows the process of transformation taking place within the National Union of Teachers, operating in England and Wales. The authors characterise this transformation as the "emergence of social movement unionism" and argue that this is both a necessary response to the challenges posed by the fragmentation of the education system, and an opportunity to develop a new form of teacher unionism, focused on organising teachers to build collective power within their workplaces and communities.

Whilst this transformation is still at its early stages and there are many bridges and hurdles to cross, the vision of a single united union, rooted in the workplace, with strong networks in local communities and a coherent analysis of neoliberalism and how to challenge it is a key goal to which the national union aspires.

This is followed by the inspiring story of another transformation: that of the Chicago Teachers' Union. In chapter ten, Carol Caref recounts the developments that led to the week and a half long Chicago teachers' strike that brought together teachers, parents and community activists in defence of their schools and their communities.

The tale of the Chicago teachers' strike has already proved an inspiration to teacher union activists across the USA and further afield, as Carol acknowledges in her paper. One of the key examples it provides is how a union can truly root its struggles in those of the wider community and act in defence of the most vulnerable children and parents. This builds on similar themes to chapter nine but takes these to a new level. There is a lesson in here for all educators that was emblazoned on the banners and placards of the mass demonstrations in downtown Chicago: our working conditions are our students learning conditions!

Chapter eleven reprints Lois Weiner's closing remarks to the conference itself, exploring the relationship between researchers and teacher union activists and how we can offer each other critical support. In particular, she looks at the crucial role of researchers in offering unions new perspectives on themselves, opportunities to learn and develop. Lois also emphasises the crucial importance in international solidarity in challenging a movement that has global reach.

The final word is given to Kristine Mayle of the Chicago Teachers' Union. Kristine presented the paper given in chapter ten at the conference and inspired delegates with her detailed analysis of how Chicago teachers challenged their own perceptions of what their union was and could be and turned this into action. So much so that she was invited to address the opening session of our Annual Conference earlier this year. It is her speech from this occasion that we reprint as an afterword as it sets out so clearly where we are and where we need to be. The fact is, we are at the forefront of a battle for the future not just of our education systems but of our societies.

As Nelson Mandela argued: 'Education is the most powerful weapon we can use to change the world."

There is an alternative to the neoliberal policies of the GERM. All over the world, teachers and parents are struggling to make this alternative a reality. I hope this book inspires you to join them.

Contributors

Hugo Aboites is Professor of Education and rector of the Autonomous University of Mexico City. He is author of numerous books and articles, including *The School as Community Hub: Beyond Education's Iron Cage*

Christine Blower is General Secretary of the National Union of Teachers and President of ETUCE, the European section of Education International. She taught from 1973 until she was elected as Deputy General Secretary and has classroom experience in both primary and secondary settings as well as Pupil Referral Units. As the grandmother of a 3 year old she fears for the future of education!

Carol Caref, research director for the Chicago Teachers Union, is the lead author of several CTU publications; the most recent is *A Just Chicago: Fighting for the City Our Students Deserve*. This report details the intimate connection of health, housing, jobs, segregation, and funding to education. Before coming to the CTU in 2010, Carol taught high school mathematics in Chicago Public Schools for 25 years. She is passionate about teaching and fighting for what students need and deserve.

Lars Dahlström is Emeritus Associate Professor of Education, Umea University. He has written and researched extensively on the effects of neoliberal education policy, particularly in the global South. His latest publications include: *You are being cheated: a critical analysis of Teach for Sweden* and *Case Studies of Teacher Education Forces in the Global South: Pedagogical possibilities when the main door is closed* (together with John Nyambe)

Angelo Gavrielatos is the Project Director at Educational International (EI) responsible for leading EI's response to the growing commercialisation and privatisation of education. He was the Federal President of the Australian Education Union (AEU) for 7 years prior to commencing work with EI. He started his career as a secondary teacher in Green valley in South West Sydney in 1987. His commitment to social justice unionism is at the heart of his work.

Edgar Isch is an academic who works closely with UNE, the union that represents teachers in Ecuador. He was environment minister in the government of Ecuador for a short time before leaving the position as a critic of the extractivist direction taken by the current government. He is a member of the Research Network of the IDEA Network that publishes research and the bilingual magazine *Intercambio*.

Larry Kuehn is Director of Research and Technology at the British Columbia Teachers' Federation in Canada. He is also responsible for the International Solidarity Program of the BCTF and writes about the impact of neo-liberal globalization on public education.

Ravi Kumar teaches at the Department of Sociology, South Asian University. His works include *Education, State and Market: Anatomy of Neoliberal Impact* (2014, Aakar Books: Delhi); *Social Movements: Transformative Shifts and Turning Points* (Forthcoming, Routledge: Delhi); *Education and the Reproduction of Capital: Neoliberal Knowledge and Counterstrategies* (2012, Palgrave Macmillan: New York)

Gawain Little teaches maths at a primary school in Oxford, UK, and is a member of the NUT's National Executive Committee. He is Chair of the NUT Professional Unity Committee, an officer of Unify – the campaign for one education union, and a member of the editorial board of *Education for Tomorrow*.

Brook Lemma is Professor at Addis Ababa University, Ethiopia. Researched, published and coordinated a masters program on Critical Practitioner Inquiry (CPI) in collaboration with professors in Umeå University, Sweden. Currently working on organizing PhD program in the same in one of the Ethiopian universities along with Professor Lars Dahlström, leading author of the article in this publication.

Maurie Mulheron is President of the New South Wales Teachers' Federation and Deputy President of the Australian Education Union. An active teacher unionist for over 30 years, he has written extensively on education policy and the impact of neoliberalism. His contribution to this book is based on a more detailed paper *If We Forget History*, published in June 2014 by the NSW Teachers' Federation.

Kristine A. Mayle is Financial secretary of the Chicago Teachers Union. She has been a special educational needs teacher in middle schools in Chicago. She was actively involved in the fight against school closures in the town. Since then she has been working for the CTU in its ongoing fight against school closures, common core, testing and for a fair contract for teachers.

Francisco Dominguez is a Senior Lecturer at Middlesex University and Head of the Latin American Studies Research Group. His publications include: 'Venezuela's opposition: desperately seeking to overthrow Chávez', in F. Dominguez, G. Lievesley and S. Ludlam (eds.) Right-Wing Politics in the New Latin America (2011); 'The Latinamericanization of the politics of emancipation', in G. Lievesley and S.Ludlam (eds.) Reclaiming Latin America: Experiments in Radical Social Democracy (2009); 'Violence, the Left and the creation of Un Nuevo Chile', in W. Fowler and P. Lambert (eds.) Political Violence and Identity in Latin America (2008); 'The rise of the private sector in Cuba', in A. Gray and A. Kapcia (eds.), The Changing Dynamics of Cuban Civil Society (2008); and F. Dominguez and M. Guedes de Oliveira (eds.) Mercosur: Between Integration and Democracy (2003).

Susan Robertson is Professor of Education at Bristol University. She has written extensively on the effects of global education 'reform' policy. She is the founding director of the Centre for Globalisation, Education and Societies. Her most recent publications include: 'Teachers' Work, Denationalisation and Transformations in the Field of Symbolic Control'. in: John Levin, Terri Seddon, Jenny Ozga (eds) *World yearbook of Education 2013*. Routledge and 'The Social Justice Implications of Privatisation in Education Governance Frameworks: A Relational Account'. *Oxford Review of Education*, vol 39., pp. 426-445

Howard Stevenson is Professor of Educational Leadership at Nottingham University. Before working in higher education, he was a teacher in a comprehensive school in Leicestershire for 15 years and an active member of the NUT. He has written extensively about the effects of current education policy on both schools and teaching unions. His latest publication is, Markets, managerialism and teachers' work: the invisible hand of high stakes testing in England *International Education Journal: Comparative Perspectives.*

Lois Weiner is Professor of Education at New Jersey University. Previously she taught in urban schools in California and New York. Her research and activism is focused on the need to democratise teaching unions and on the effects of the global assault of neo-liberal education 'reform'. She is the author of numerous articles and several books, most recently, *The Future of our Schools: Teachers Unions and Social Justice* 2014 Haymarket Books

1 What teachers need to know about the 'Global Education Reform Movement' (or GERM)

Susan L Robertson

WHEN SUCH a staunch advocate for testing, accountability and Charter Schools in the United States – Diane Ravitch – declared in 2010 that these education policies had all been a big mistake – we know something serious is afoot. After all, it is not often that an organic intellectual of the political right publicly declares that those policies they had been instrumental in shaping have, as things turn out, been particularly damaging to America's schools.

To make matters worse, Pasi Sahlberg, points out that the poster country for the OECD's Programme for International Student Assessment (PISA), Finland, is a top performing country precisely because they don't have in place what he refers to as the Global Education Reform Movement policies – or GERM. Rather – Finland has managed to deliver an excellent education for students NOT going down the path of standardisation, student testing, accountability and competition. And indeed Sahlberg (2012) argues that ".healthy schools are resistant to GERM and its inconvenient symptoms". Furthermore, he adds, 'In these countries, teaching remains an attractive career choice for young people".

Yet this has not acted as a wake-up call to a range of nationally and internationally located education policy entrepreneurs – including government departments, the (OECD), the World Bank, education philanthropic groups, education consultancy firms, education corporations, and private equity investors, all actively promoting this particular policy suite around the globe.

Instead, if anything, there has been a ramping up of the GERM policies. Which of course leads to the very obvious question. Why? Why would someone set out to deliberately make our education system ill? Is this a case of neglect, or ignorance, or are other interests at work?

In this chapter I try to answer these questions, arguing we have an open debate about what the evidence is showing us, and that this evidence is important in building the kind of education institutions that are more able to deliver a high quality learning and teaching experience. I want to begin, first, by looking more closely at the detail of the Global Education Reform Movement policies and what the evidence is as to their outcomes for producing high quality teaching and learning environments.

The DNA of GERM – neoliberalism

Pasi Sahlberg has written extensively on the global education reform movement, GERM, arguing that its genesis can be traced to the Education Reform Act, launched in 1988 in

Margaret Thatcher's England (Sahlberg, 2011: 174). Four elements characterised this reform: that public sectors like education could, and should, be governed using ideas drawn from a market economy. These were competition (between schools), autonomy (such as devolution), choice (parents to decide where the child goes to school) and information (so that choices can be made based on student and school performance).

Yet these four elements were not ideas specific to the reorganisation of public education. Rather, they emerged from the advance of an ideological project that was able to gain considerable traction in political circles in the 1980s following the global economic crisis in the 1970s throwing into doubt Keynesian economic theory. Key proponents included the Viennese economist, Friedrich Hayek, and the Chicago-based economist, Milton Friedman. Both had spent a considerable amount of time since 1947 critiquing welfare-based democracies. And as the late historian, Eric Hobsbawm (1994: 409) observed of the time:

> The battle between Keynesians and neo-liberals was...a war of incompatible ideologies... Keynesians claimed that high wages, full employment and the Welfare State created the consumer demand that had fuelled expansion, and that pumping more demand into the economy was the best way to deal with economic depressions. The neo-liberals argued that ... Adam Smith's 'hidden hand' of the free market was bound to produce the greatest growth of the 'Wealth of Nations' and the best sustainable distribution of wealth and income within it.

Neo-liberalisms' pedigree can be traced to liberalism; a utopian project promoted by philosophers such as Locke and Hobbes, committed to the ideals of personal freedom and possessive individualism (Macpherson, 1962: 263-4). But most importantly, liberalism stood opposed to collectivism. The core ideas of liberalism are outlined by Macpherson; freedom from dependence on others, the individual is the proprietor of his own person and capacities; human societies consist of a series of market relations; and political society is constructed to protect an individual's property and goods. In other words, supreme value is given to individual autonomy, agency and property. These ideas were, in turn, deployed to radically refashion a growing number of societies around the globe into 'market societies', as well as their public services, like education, into 'market-looking' services. Colin Leys calls these initiatives, 'market-driven politics' (2001).

As I have argued elsewhere (Robertson, 2008), political projects need more than proposers to propagate and prosper. They also need various groups to buy into, and own, this set of ideas. And indeed neo-liberalism had sufficiently broad appeal—particularly in the idea of individual freedom. Neo-liberalism was able to articulate with a range of interests, discourses and agendas within civil society that had been submerged. In the USA, for example, neo-liberal ideology spoke to those groups and communities for example, the Christian Right, liberal feminists and black communities, whose identities and projects had been previously denied by the post-war white male class project (Apple, 2001).

In the UK, Margaret Thatcher offered to chart a course out of the difficult days that surrounded the 1970s crisis, by challenging 'creeping socialism', on the one hand,

and promising law, order, social discipline and authority, on the other (Hall, 1979: 16). The discourse of 'rights' was also mobilised as a means to realise freedom through opening up previously dominated state spheres to other actors, in essence offering the very real possibility of setting up new institutional structures, this time using a using a market-based rationale (for instance, Charter Schools, Academies, and so on). Neo-liberal policies also resonated amongst the ruling classes who had been forced into a taxation regime that promoted welfare based redistribution policies. Neo-liberalism was thus perfect economic engine to drive forward this project.

Global education reform movement policies have neoliberalism in their DNA – and that is what makes them particularly problematic for those concerned with education. In other words, viewing education, and the relationship between the teacher and the learning, the family and the school, in market terms badly distorts the idea of 'education' itself. To 'educate' is to give intellectual, moral and social instruction to another. It does not mean viewing the individual's 'education' like any kind of bar-coded product to be scanned at the supermarket and checked for whether its contents fit the standard specified on the tin.

Placing the GERM under the microscope

Sahlberg (2011: 177-179) outlines six global features of the global education reform movement that he argues characterises many education systems around the world.

Feature One: *an over-preoccupation with standardization in and of education*. The belief here is that by setting clear and high standards of performance for students, teachers and schools, this will lead to improvements in the quality of outcomes. This in itself is not an issue – as standards are important. But the fetishization with standards as an end in itself leads to an unhealthy diet of centralised curriculum and assessment programmes, accompanied by constant target setting and monitoring. This in turn leads to teaching to the test and the homogenisation of learning; quite the opposite to the desired outcomes.

Feature Two: an over-preoccupation with literacy and numeracy. That is, basic knowledge in the subjects – mathematics, literacy, science – that has, in the hands of the OECD, been closely aligned to economic performance. When linked to an unhealthy preoccupation with standards as outlined above, this not only weights the curriculum towards these areas, but in doing so, offers the student a lop-sided education experience. This in turn sets up a new problem. In ignoring the arts and humanities, we are in effect ignoring a well-spring for creativity and innovation that is essential for thinking about contribution a good education can make to shaping imaginative and sustainable futures.

Feature Three: *a preoccupation with pre-determined results*. The combination of standardisation (feature one) in core areas of performance (feature two), in turn attracts system approval or disapproval, and hardly surprisingly results in teachers and student searching for safe, low risk strategies that don't attract unwarranted attention. Of course the commercial world is on standby, willing to 'sell' the latest idea as a sure fire solution. Sahlberg talks about 'proven methods' and 'guaranteed content' as some of the signifiers here. And of course this feeds very nicely into the commercial firms who are ready and waiting to offer the latest solution guaranteed not to fail. Yet, quality teaching and learning must not only be experimental in its attitude, but it is precisely this attribute that is likely to lead to innovative and creative solutions to the problems of our time.

Feature Four: a preoccupation with innovation from the corporate to the educational world. The main idea here is that the corporate world has far better insights into what and how students learn, teachers' teach, and schools become excellent. By learning from this world, or indeed enabling this corporate world to act as managers of education institutions and providers of education, then the quality of education will be superior. This kind of idea is widely supported by international organisations like the World Bank, as well as those who stand to gain by creating education into a sector where significant profits can be made. It also leads to the undermining of teacher learning and capacity building so as to better respond to the specificities of learners and the social contexts.

Feature Five: a preoccupation with test-based accountability policies. Here the focus is on accountability, and how the outputs (test results) of students are then used as the basis for determining the success of failure of the teacher and the school. When teacher pay, for instance, or teacher promotion, is linked to student test scores – as in value added measures, an assumption being made that an individual teacher is *responsible for individual pupil learning. A wide range of other variables might well be at work as to the causes of pupil learning gains; these include wider social and economic factors, developmental factors, and so on.*

Feature Six: a preoccupation with the increased control of schools. A wide range of measures in place – audits, standards, teacher proof curriculum, external assessments, and so on all suggest that teachers cannot be trusted to use their professional expertise in making judgements about teaching and learning. In those systems where GERM policies are in place the lack of trust in teachers has had damaging consequences for education; on teacher recruitment is difficult and teacher retention problematic – in turn undermining quality learning experiences. The dependence on unqualified teachers, on the one hand, or teachers drawn from the temporary supply pool, on the other, destabilise learning, as well as undermine the capacity of a school to build a shared pool of knowledge around pupils, learning outcomes, and their wider social-economic contexts.

Now at this point you are rightly asking about the evidence. Not to worry. There is plenty. But it is the evidence from Sahlberg (2011: 181-183) on Finland in particular, and GERM countries more generally, that is compelling, largely as it presents us with a rather inconvenient truth. GERM countries like the USA, England, Canada and New Zealand all combine a combination of choice, competition, information and accountability in their policy mix for governing schools. The overall trend, Sahlberg points out, is for a declining level of performance on PISA measures in mathematics. Finland was the only country to show a consistent level of improvement, and it is one of the few countries that does not have GERM policies in place. But what it does have are policies that value teachers, and places high value on teacher professionalism and judgement, rewards teachers properly financially. More than this, this long standing commitment to system wide improvement over time has also resulted in system-wide equity. Those who are keen to poor cold water on the Finnish exception argue that Finland is indeed exceptional because it is a small, relatively homogeneous, society. However this is unlikely to be a cause of Finland's success in securing ongoing sustainable reform.

If GERM policies are bad for learners and teachers, then who benefits?

By now you likely have a sense as to what the answer to this question is from what I have been saying so far. I've not argued that standards, or accountability, or a concern with competences in mathematics, literacy, or science, are bad. Far from it. Like Sahlberg, my view is likely to accord with most teachers, and that it is the *over-preoccupation* with these elements, at the expense of a more well-rounded education, that is the issue. So if an excess of standardisation, testing, auditing and control are bad for learners and teachers, who, then is it good for?

Consider this fact. In estimating the value of education globally, a report in 2014 by investors working for Merrill Lynch Bank of America valued it at $4.3 trillion. Who were to be the beneficiaries of this? The Report stated that three large global publishing companies would be the main beneficiaries of education profits into the future. Pearson Education, Elsevier and Informa! Now of course the publishing world has always had a strong foot in education – whether in schools, colleges or universities, through their interests in textbook production, journals, and so on. But these firms are not imagining themselves as operating on the margins – but increasingly moving into core business, or engaged in shaping the education sector as well as institutional fortunes and teacher careers in significant ways.

But firms like Pearson see big opportunities in developing their edu-business portfolio. Pearson owns the *Financial Times*; they also own the examination company EdExcel which services English schools. More recently Pearson Education established a for-profit university in London, and helped finance a chain of low fee private schools in Ghana. Pearson Education also collects different data sets together on aspects of learning and publishes what it calls The Learning Curve. Here countries can see at a glance how well they are performing on a range of 'learning measures'. The OECD's Andreas Schleicher also sits on the steering committee of Pearson's Learning Curve, suggesting a close alignment of the OECD with Pearson Education.

Huge issues immediately present themselves to us, for firms like these have made their money from scaling up, creating new demand where none exists, and generating mass markets. That we might imagine a world of education that is dominated by transnational firms – active from the USA to India, England to Ghana with a one size fits all 'school in a box' offer – suggests that different science traditions, pedagogies, learning styles and so on, are what is at stake.

Now consider this fact. In 2011, the first ever *International Summit on the Teaching Profession* convened in New York in 2011. Significantly, the OECD

Director of the Indicators and Analysis Division, Andreas Schleicher, was engaged to write the background report for the Summit, and played a leading role as 'framer' of the agenda. The background report – *Building a High Quality Teaching Profession: Lessons from Around the World* (OECD 2011) considered evidence around issues of teacher recruitment, ongoing learning, and professional development, how teachers were evaluated and compensated, and the ways teachers engaged in reform. But what was particularly disturbing was the solutions being proposed by Schleicher; those policies that both Ravitch and Sahlberg show have been particularly detrimental to creating quality teaching and learning experiences. And despite Schleicher arguing that it is teachers who need to be involved in these conversations, as it is they who make the decisions on the ground, they were no-where to be seen in the Summit.

Observe also the paradox here of the OECD's own position in the world of education – as a shaper of students' and teachers' work from on high with a narrow 'one size fits all' solution to education. And it is precisely this; that the OECD has become a loud and powerful voice in the shaping of what counts as teaching and learning, and what its role and purpose should be in our societies, rather than involving those whom it makes responsible for the outcomes. Yet the OECD benefits precisely as it uses education to advance its own position of power in the pantheon of global governance institutions, whilst at the same time advancing the interests of those economic classes whom it serves.

Finally, consider this fact. The Bill and Melinda Gates Foundation have put close to $1/3rd billion on the table to look at teacher effectiveness and value-added measures in the United States. Value added approaches aim to measure the value that a teacher adds to the student's learning having taught the student in (mathematics, science, reading, and so on). Corporate philanthropists and their Foundations, the Walmart Foundation, Lumina Foundation, Bill and Melinda Gates Foundation, the Robertson Foundation, the Broad Foundation, William and Flora Hewlett Foundation – the list goes on – are increasingly targeting their contributions to education – often in the form of securing tax breaks – in areas of education policymaking and programme intervention so as to hugely shape the direction of the sector. And whilst philanthropic organisations are not new kids on the block when it comes to education, in the past they tended to be more altruistic and liberal in their approach to education. More recently, researchers show that Foundations are interested in promoting particular governance models in education, such as charter schools, school vouchers, standards and testing – and are promoting a strong vision for education and for learners (as passionate entrepreneurs). But again the bigger issue here is not so much that this money is not welcome, but it gives the Foundations significantly more influence over shaping policy making process than the wider community, including the education community.

GERM: a bundle of contradictions and paradoxes

The GERM suite of policies is full of contradictions and paradoxes: wanting to create potentially innovative workers, yet driving out opportunities for creativity in learners because of reinforcing risk aversion and narrowing the 'valued' curriculum; wanting to promote high levels of performance and quality in teachers and learners but tending toward homogeneity and uniformity through centralised control over the curriculum, assessment and pedagogy; viewing teachers as part of the problem, but also part of the solution; arguing that education is an important human right and building block for the future, whilst privileging the market and its interests in the education sector. The list goes on. All this, of course, suggests that the global education reforms that have bitten deeply into, and transformed many of our education systems, is simply not up to the task of creating the kinds of learning opportunities and institutions that will make the right kind of difference. Educators, and those concerned about the future of education, need to take a stand and demand a different set of conversations.

Let's 'stand up' for a different kind of 'education' than the GERM offers

We need to ask bigger questions around what is kind of education will best serve our societies in the 21st century that do not have a narrow-minded set of answers as a response. Can we pose more imaginative questions and insist on more imaginative answers? Experience consistently tells us, if we look around, that the conditions for human flourishing and ongoing sustainability are drawn – not from a narrowing down – but a diversity of knowledges, experiences, epistemologies, ways of learning, ways of knowing. In short, let's stand up for the kind of education that challenges the logics of GERM and which offers the promise of a rather different present and future.

References

Apple, M. (2001) *Comparing neoliberal projects and inequality in education*, Comparative Education, 37 (4), pp. 409-23.

Hall, S. (1979) The great moving right show, *Marxism Today*, January, pp. 14-120.

Hobsbawm, E. (1994). *Age of Extremes: the Short Twentieth Century 1914-91*, London: Abacus.

Leys, C. (2001) *Market-Driven Politics: Neoliberal Democracy and the Public Interest*, London: Verso.

Macpherson, C. B. (1962) *The Political Theory of Possessive Individualism: Hobbes to Locke*, Oxford: Oxford at the Clarendon Press.

Merrill Lynch Bank of America (2014) A transforming world, The Thundering Word, [http://corp.bankofamerica.com/documents/16303/855792/The_Thundering_Word_Macro Themes_Report_043014.pdf – last accessed 14th April 2015].

OECD. 2011. OECD Teaching and Learning International Survey (TALIS) TALIS 2013, Paris: OECD [at http://www.oecd.org/document/40/0,4746,en_2649 – last accessed 10 April 2015].

Ravitch, (2010). *The Death and Life of the Great American School System: How Testing and Choice Are Undermining Education*, New York: Basic Books.

Riep, C., (2013) Omega schools franchise in Ghana: 'affordable' private education for the poor or profiteering, in I. Macpherson, S. Robertson and G. Walford (eds.). *Education, Privatisation and Social Justice: Case Studies from South Asia and South East Asia*, Didcot, UK: Symposium Books.

Robertson, S. (2008) Remaking the world: Neoliberalism, and the transformation of education and teachers' labour, in M. Compton and L. Weiner, (eds.) *The Global Assault Teaching, Teachers and their Unions*, Basingstoke: Palgrave.

Robertson, S. (2012) Placing teachers in global governance agendas, *Comparative Education Review*, 56 (3), November, pp. 377-406.

Sahlberg, P (2011) The fourth way of Finland, in *Journal of Educational Change*, 12, pp. 173-85.

Schleicher, Andreas and Vivian Stewart. 2009. Benchmarking, Asia Society, [http://asiasociety.org/education/learning-world/international-benchmarking – last accessed 10th April 2015].

2 The impact of the USA and UK on public education in Australia

Maurie Mulheron

THIS ARTICLE outlines why Australian public school systems have been affected by global 'education reforms' and is based on a longer and more detailed paper, *If We Forget History*, published in June 2014.

When Australia became a federation in 1901, the new constitution ensured that public education would remain the responsibility of the six state and two federal territory governments. Over the decades, the states lost a great deal of their revenue raising capacity to the federal government but retained the responsibilities for large portfolio areas such as education, transport and health. However, due to political pressure, the federal government assumed responsibility for significant funding of the private (non-government) schooling sector from the 1970s onwards.

The current enrolment share is 66% of students attend public (government) schools and 34% attend private schools. Of this latter group, 20% are enrolled in Catholic private schools and 14% in other, mainly religious, private schools. Until the recent review into schools funding, the private sector received approximately 70% of federal school funding plus significant funding from state governments as well. Their income is also supplemented by charging fees. As such, they have an enormous financial advantage over the government system.

Each state and territory has a single union that covers all teachers, including principals, in the public education system. Each state based union is affiliated to the national teachers' union, the Australian Education Union (AEU).

Even before the introduction of neo-liberal educational policies, Australian education has been characterised by deep inequalities reflecting broader social disadvantage but exacerbated by deliberate policy settings that are designed to favour private schooling. The key feature of Australian schooling is that it is highly segregated with a large percentage of socially disadvantaged students, and massive gaps in achievement between rich and poor of up to four to six years of schooling. As the social gap widens, public schools are doing the 'heavy lifting' in education but are vastly under-resourced for the challenges.

Funding policies introduced decades ago have meant that private schools in Australia receive the majority of federal schools funding, including huge grants for capital works. At the state level, they receive additional funding. On top of this, the private sector has the right to charge uncapped fees and have retained total autonomy as to which students they choose to enrol. The result is that the public education system with the most students with complex needs has been seriously undermined due to funding policies.

Relatively recent OECD studies have shown Australia to be a low equity nation in the resourcing of schools because the country has amongst the largest disparities in the resources available to low and high socio-economic (SES) schools across the OECD.

This difference between low and high SES schools in Australia in the quality of educational resources is the fifth largest in the OECD. [1]

Additional OECD data also shows that the difference in the quality of physical infrastructure between low and high SES schools in Australia is also amongst the highest in the OECD. [2]

Australia has a higher concentration of disadvantaged students enrolled in schools with a low socio-economic status. Almost every one of these schools is within the public system. Almost 60% of the most disadvantaged students are enrolled in these schools. This level of *concentration* of disadvantage is substantially higher than in any comparable OECD country. [3]

The ideology of choice has driven funding policies for decades. As a result, Australia has the highest degree of school choice of any OECD country leading to concentrations of disadvantage, low equity and social segregation. 90% of students are enrolled in secondary schools that compete with two or more schools, as reported by principals. This compares to the OECD average of 60%. [4]

"Choice has not enlarged the educational opportunities of the poor. Indeed the tendency for choice to segregate children in the lower bands of socio-economic status has created worsening conditions for the populations who most depend on the effectiveness of public schools. Growth in public and private spending in the non-government sector has operated to remove more culturally advantaged children and young people from the public systems, leaving these systems less supported culturally by a balanced mix of students from different family backgrounds." [5]

So, Australian public education, already under enormous strain due to huge funding disparities, has in recent years been hit with a set of neo-liberal policies designed to permanently weaken the system.

Why Australia?

Perhaps if the French explorer, Jean-François de Galaup La Pérouse, had been a little less tardy in arriving at Botany Bay, New South Wales, in late January 1788, Australian teachers today may have been spared the worst of a range of educational 'reforms' that dominate much of the policy formations throughout the English speaking world. Australian politicians spent most of the last hundred years or more making sure Australia followed either Great Britain or the United States of America (USA) into their military conflicts, from the Boer War to Iraq and Afghanistan. And so it should be no surprise that, when it comes to the 'education wars' of the last thirty years, the habits of slavish adherence to the doctrines of these two countries would continue.

Much of what passes as educational policy in Australia is imported from either the United Kingdom (UK) or the USA, sometimes with the obligatory footnote acknowledging the source, but mostly plagiarised. If we have learned anything about globalisation it is that national boundaries are mostly irrelevant as large corporations, with no geographic centre, or indeed national loyalty, can now purchase policy and policy makers just about anywhere, notwithstanding phone hacking scandals that sometimes expose their spheres of influence.

The role played by these two influential English speaking countries was to develop national education policy settings that would reflect, serve and be subordinate to dominant neo-liberal economic doctrines. International agencies and inter-governmental bodies ensured that what had started as national agendas, created by politically conservative governments, would change education systems all around the world, with few countries spared.

Confronted with a new policy enthusiasm that, more often than not, bears no relation to their reality, teachers in Australia could not be blamed for asking: Who thought of that? Why us?

It is worth gaining some understanding the origins of educational policy in both the USA and the UK and why to this day this still influences policy makers in Australia. The broader global education agenda is based on the contention that educational improvement will evolve by competition and the application of market forces through parental choice along with business management and performance accountability mechanisms. The speed at which the ideology shifts across borders has been described as an 'epidemic'.[6]

Heavily influenced by large corporations, dominant media players and conservative think-tanks, using a new managerial language from a lexicography compiled by business schools, political parties implement policies that are designed to end the 'state monopoly'. No matter what the service, and often in defiance of public opinion, this ideology is applied to public provision including postal and communication services, transport, roads, shipping ports, airports, health care, welfare, prisons, security services, employment services, housing, utilities such as water and energy and, of course, education.

The global conservative agenda for public education appears complex and all-encompassing with so many fronts having opened up. Australian teachers would recognise many of the elements of this agenda that includes:
- The fragmentation and privatisation of the public school system through Charter Schools, Academies, Trust Schools, Free Schools, and the creation of specialist and selective schools;
- The devolution agenda, marketed under a variety of names such as 'school-based management', 'school autonomy', 'independent public schools', or 'principal empowerment', that heralds the destruction of education departments and the loss of systemic support for schools;
- Funding cuts to public schools, growth in vouchers and the proliferation of government funded private providers and contestable funding models;
- The high stakes testing agenda, 'league tables', the stigmatising of public schools, school closures, teacher and principal sackings;
- The politicisation of school curriculum, sidelining the professional voice of teachers and marginalising certain subjects;
- Loss of tenure, permanency and the growth in precarious employment in teaching;
- Teacher salary cuts and wage freezes reinforced by 'performance', 'bonus' or 'merit' pay;

● An direct attack on teaching qualifications exemplified in programs such as Teach for All, including a Teach for Australia franchise, that grew out of Teach for America;
● Employing non-educators in leadership positions in schools and in positions within education departments;
● The demonising of public school teachers and their unions; and,
● The phenomenal rise of 'edu-businesses' that have crossed a line from selling education resources to now establishing for-profit school systems.

But underpinning all of this is a deeply held belief that there is little role for government to play in providing services to the public. As the former Australian Federal Minister for Schools, David Kemp, argued, 'If you can find suppliers of a particular service in the Yellow Pages [phone directory] you may ask: why is the government providing it."[7] It is not surprising that at the same time that he was education minister, Kemp was also Minister Assisting the Minister for Finance for Privatisation.

In developing our understanding of what is happening in Australia, it would be useful to explore the political origins of the so-called 'education reform' agenda, or as Pasi Sahlberg the Finnish educator describes it, the Global Education Reform Movement or G.E.R.M. Why did Australia get infected?

Why is it that our public school systems in so many countries, including Australia, have been subjected to perpetual criticism and radical experimentation? The short answer is that opponents of public provision used neo-liberal economic orthodoxies and 'new public sector management' theory to develop education policies that reflected, not the three 'Rs', but new priorities – the three 'Ms', markets, managers and measurement.

As a starting point, we should visit the USA in the era of Ronald Reagan, the 1980s, before crossing the Atlantic to Thatcher's Britain. Most of the ideas that are now dominating educational policy in Australia emanate from a time of leg-warmers, shoulder pads and parachute pants; when The Captain and Tennille's hit single *Do That To Me One More Time* topped the charts, when Cats was about to open in the West End and *The Empire Strikes Back* was packing them into cinemas everywhere.

An empire at risk

"If an unfriendly foreign power had attempted to impose on America the mediocre educational performance that exists today, we might have well viewed it as an act of war."[8]

There appears to be a common modus operandi adopted by 'education reformers' in whatever jurisdiction they operate. At first, there is the requirement to establish as a truth that there is an educational crisis. The crisis becomes a permanent state of affairs. This misuse of student assessment data is critical to the success of the neo-liberal agenda. Public enterprises cannot be seen to be successful. High stakes testing provides an endless source of data for this purpose.

But what if education standards have not been in steady decline? What if the need for an 'education reform' movement was based on faulty evidence? What if the educational crisis was actually manufactured? What if most major 'reforms' that have been foisted on public schools in Australia and other countries in recent decades were based on lies?

There seems to be widespread acceptance that 1983 was a watershed year in the debate about 'falling standards' with the publication of *A Nation at Risk: The Imperative for Educational Reform*. This is the title of the report of U.S. President Ronald Reagan's National Commission on Excellence in Education. Despite it being a short paper 36 pages in length, it is arguably the most influential report on education ever written in the USA. Its impact is still being felt today, not only in the USA, but across the world.

In essence, the Commission was charged with the responsibility for assessing the quality of teaching and learning at elementary, secondary and tertiary levels. As well, the Commission was to compare American schools and colleges with other advanced nations. This second priority was of deep political significance, born during the post-war period in US history.

What distinguished the *A Nation at Risk* report from earlier reports was its language and tone. Reagan's Secretary of Education, Terrell Howard Bell, hired professional writers. Consequently, its pages were peppered with emotive language, hyperbole and rhetorical flourishes. Terms such as 'rising tide of mediocrity', 'act of war' and 'threatens our very future' were just purpose-made for headline writers.

"The educational foundations of our society are presently being eroded by a rising tide of mediocrity that threatens our very future as a Nation and a people."

The very words in the title of the report, 'a nation at risk', exploited national insecurity,

"Our nation is at risk. Our once unchallenged pre-eminence in commerce, industry, science, and technological innovation is being overtaken by our competitors throughout the world..."

Apart from its extraordinary use of language, it was the first significant report that triggered a response from some that questioned the very existence of public schools. It can be argued that public schools in the USA have been in retreat ever since. This is why it is such a far-reaching report.

As could be expected, the initial responses to the report, however, were calls for additional resources. But these voices were drowned out by others who called for a radical restructuring of the US schooling system. These groups developed a broader agenda based on the contention that educational improvement would evolve by competition and the application of market forces through parental choice underpinned by business management and performance accountability mechanisms.

What is surprising about the report is its lack of academic rigour. Much of the report is anecdotal and rhetorical, as can be seen from this extract:

"History is not kind to idlers. The time is long past when American's destiny was assured simply by an abundance of natural resources and inexhaustible human enthusiasm, and by our relative isolation from the malignant problems of older civilizations."

A Nation at Risk claimed that Scholastic Aptitude Test (SAT) scores had declined during the period analysed. It was a central claim that shocked America, vindicating, it would appear, the critics of public schools.

Reagan went on to make over fifty 'time-to-get-tough-on-education' speeches during his second term of office. The media fell into line, generally uncritically, running hundreds of stories across the country upon release of the report. [9] Over 500,000 copies of the report were distributed and within four months of its release, it had become the subject of over 700 articles in 45 major newspapers. [10]

A Nation at Risk was able to shift the blame for the economic, political and social crises facing America to one institution, public education. It was spectacularly successful in scapegoating teachers and public schools. There is very little wonder that political conservatives and corporate America formed an alliance that has endured to this day.

However, there was one problem. A Nation at Risk had essentially got it wrong. Its fundamental premise that test scores had declined would eventually be challenged. However, the nature of the challenge and the reaction to it highlights the intensely political nature of the 'education reform' agenda.

Perhaps because much of the content of A Nation at Risk was couched in terms that related to threats to national security, it is not surprising that an institution that was part of the US military-industrial complex would take an interest in the report.

Scientists at the Sandia National Laboratory in Albuquerque, New Mexico, were commissioned to find the hard data missing from the original report which would document and prove the decline in educational standards. It seemed a straightforward task and so the engineers at Sandia analysed the SAT data.

When the Sandia scientists broke down the previously aggregated data into sub-groups based on poverty, ethnicity, ability and wealth, a very different picture emerged. Almost every sub-group either improved or stayed constant. The data showed no decline at all. What was happening? Why had the overall average scores declined while each sub-group had either improved or remained steady?

The statisticians at Sandia knew the answer. It is called Simpson's paradox. While the average scores can head in one direction, the scores of each sub-group can move in the opposite direction. Once only top ranking students completed high school. As retention rates increased over time, more students were taking the SAT tests. Proportionally, therefore, the number of top performing students was smaller, and so the average scores dropped. There was no decline after all as measured by the SAT tests, just many more students from much wider backgrounds sitting for the tests.

But rather than be greeted as the bearers of good news, the Sandia engineers were pressured not to release the 156-page 1990 Sandia Report. From this point on test data would become the weapon of choice to ensure that public schools, and the teachers working within them, would be forever on the defensive.

It became a strategy that conservative politicians were pleased to employ and to export.

The risk spreads

At about the same time as the release of A Nation at Risk, UNESCO had been promised funding from the World Bank to develop a new range of educational indicators. Given UNESCO's work across the globe, particularly in developing countries, there was an expectation that these new indicators would be very broad and include a range of social and cultural measures that would give a context to educational achievement.

An early international test called the Secondary International Maths and Science Study (SIMMS) had been cited in *A Nation at Risk*. The Reagan administration, now keenly aware of the power of test data and the extent to which it could be used for political purposes, intervened. Reagan was now adamant that any educational indicators be measured in ways that would support the central thesis of *A Nation at Risk*. And, of course, the central thesis of *A Nation at Risk* was that the hegemony of the US as an economic and military power was under threat and that public schools were to blame.

As Larry Kuehn has argued, "*A Nation at Risk* kicked off a new direction in international testing studies."[11] Reagan and Margaret Thatcher, the British Prime Minister who was extraordinarily close to the US President, pressured UNESCO to adopt an international testing regime that would link education to economic purpose and emphasise accountability and performance rather than inputs and process. What motivated them was the political need to blame the education system for the economic malaise of both countries. A Nation at Risk had provided the original argument. However, UNESCO, governed by a council made up of member nations, refused.

The US went on to pull out of UNESCO in 1984 with the UK withdrawing the following year. Both nations also withdrew their funding of UNESCO, crippling many of its programs.

Both the USA and the UK now turned to the OECD (Organisation for Economic Co-operation and Development) to undertake the development of the international tests. There was some initial reluctance but most countries capitulated following threats from the USA and the UK that they would withdraw from it as well.

"*By the mid 80s, the US changed its role in the educational collaboration of the OECD from passivity to aggressive missionary activities ... This policy was pursued with ... attacks upon the education sector within the OECD Council...*"[12]

This shift to OECD accountability, where market theory mechanisms were applied to public policy in general and to education in particular, meant that the purpose and effect of data collection underwent a profound change. Educational data collection was to serve an economic imperative. After all, the central "mission" of the OECD is to ensure that governments establish, "... healthy public finances as a basis of sustainable economic growth" and to "restore confidence in markets and the institutions and companies that make them function."[13]

Thatcher's Government was highly influenced by what was happening in the USA and within the OECD as a result of the close political connections between the Reagan and Thatcher. It would only be a matter of time before these two powerful English speaking nations would influence policy settings in countries like Australia. A 'global education reform movement' was now in its embryonic stage but soon began to dominate educational policies around the world, particularly among the member nations of the OECD. A political consensus was achieved as well with ideas around 'school autonomy', 'teacher performance' and 'accountability' influencing the policies of mainstream political parties in many of these countries.

> "Education is viewed primarily as an economic factor and one of the prime producers of human capital. The OECD has been a primary link in both the policy borrowing process and in promoting the new managerialism in education." [14]

The falling educational standards narrative was now dominating all discussions. The voices of teachers were rarely heard.

The mother country

In 1979, Margaret Thatcher was elected Prime Minister. A fierce and uncompromising ideologue, she set about changing Britain forever. Her policies were founded on a belief in the right-wing ideology of an unfettered market, the privatisation of state enterprises, the deregulation of financial institutions and opposition to labour rights and organised trade unionism. It was inevitable that it was only a matter of time before she turned her sights on the British education system.

> "...the twin aims of Margaret Thatcher's education policies in the 1980s were to convert the nation's schools system from a public service into a market, and to transfer power from local authorities to central government." [15]

Thatcher's first Education Secretary, Mark Carlisle, was replaced in late 1981 by Keith Joseph, a former barrister, who was on the extreme right-wing of the British Conservatives. He essentially was driven by a belief in monetarist policies and in 1974, along with Margaret Thatcher, had established a right-wing think tank called the Centre for Policy Studies which advocated for schools to be 'autonomous'. It was an institute heavily influenced by the economic theories of Milton Friedman. In a speech in 1976 that has become well known as the Stockton Lecture, *Monetarism is Not Enough*, he argued that the economy was divided between the 'wealth producers' [16] and the 'wealth consumers'. State education was clearly a 'wealth consumer'. In many respects, it was Keith Joseph who was the first to articulate what has become known as 'Thatcherism'.

In 1986, Thatcher appointed Kenneth Baker as Secretary of State for Education. Thatcher commanded Baker to change the system and gave him a month or two to devise the policies and the strategies. Baker set about the task of changing the school system with some enthusiasm unburdened by any knowledge but very aware of how the politics should be played. The void created by an absence of any serious theoretical basis for the changes was filled by political ideology, motivated by hostility towards teachers and an enduring hatred of comprehensive schooling. During this period, Baker introduced dramatic and permanent changes, all highly political and experimental- standardised testing, league tables, standardised assessment, parental 'choice' and the 'local management' of schools and a much strengthened ministry. As his interviewer commented some years later,

> "On the face of it, a reform of schools would have to have, as its overriding priority, the welfare of children. Since this involved the construction of a new system to disseminate learning and knowledge, it would have to be built on a

particularly strong intellectual foundation, a great deal of solid research and clear thinking. Not so. The most sweeping educational reforms this century, it transpires, had just as much to do with guesswork, personal whim and bare knuckle politics." [17]

By 1988, with the introduction of the Education Reform Act, power and influence over what happened in schools was wrested from Local Educational Authorities and retained by Downing Street,

"Conservative legislation sought to drive neo-liberal principles into the heart of public policy. An emphasis on cost reduction, privatisation and deregulation was accompanied by vigorous measures against the institutional bases of Conservatism's opponents, and the promotion of new forms of public management. The outcome of these processes was a form of governance in which market principles were advanced at the same time as central authority was strengthened." [18]

The real aim of 'local management' was to devolve budgets to the school level. Thatcher was a monetarist who wanted to dramatically and permanently reduce expenditure in all areas of government. Passing control of school budgets to the school level would prove to be the mechanism, the masterstroke.

"The freedom which LMS (Local Management of Schools] was supposed to offer schools was, in practice, largely illusory...For the government, LMS served three purposes: it was an important element in the creation of an education market; it took financial control away from the local authorities; and it enabled the government to 'pass the buck' to the schools when budgets were cut – as they were from the second year of LMS onwards. Indeed, school budgets were cut on six of the eight years following 1988." [19]

Any hope that British Labour upon returning to power in May 1997 might reverse the damage was short-lived. New Labour's education policies were driven by the same old ideology of 'choice and diversity'. Selective and specialist schools continued to be established to undermine comprehensive education. Blair reflected the same antipathy towards comprehensive schools as had the Conservatives. Labour began to complete the privatisation agenda established by Thatcher. Tony Blair's belief in market forces was as strident as Thatcher's so much so that the joke at the time was that Blair should have been regarded as Thatcher's greatest achievement.

Under Blair the Tory agenda continued. Schools were named, shamed and closed. More academically selective schools were announced. Privatisation was encouraged. Business became more involved and previous local authority roles were handed to private companies. 'Public/private' partnerships were created. An expanded role for churches and charities in education provision was encouraged. Under Blair, England's education system became even more of a marketplace with the opening of a plethora of competing religious schools, private schools, grammar schools, specialist schools, beacon schools, church schools, foundation schools, academies and so on.

So extreme has been agenda that has unfolded over the last three decades that the current British Government has taken the next 'logical' step: to argue for the full privatisation of schooling and for schools to be run on a for-profit basis.

Visits to the antipodes

Margaret Thatcher visited Australia five times including three times during her 11 year term as Prime Minister. No other British Prime Minister has visited Australia on so many occasions. The relationship between the UK Conservative Party and its Australian counterpart, the Liberal Party, is deep.

But it is the visit to Australia of her Secretary for Education, Kenneth Baker, in autumn of 1989 that is of some interest. Baker had been invited to deliver a keynote address at an education conference in Sydney organised for May 10 of that year by the influential right-wing think tank, the Institute of Public Affairs (IPA). The IPA is one of the groups that had founded the Liberal Party back in the 1940s and has always had close ties with UK Tories. It has powerful corporate backers.

Baker began his speech with false humility, 'I should say at once that my reforms are not designed for export. They arise from the particular history and stage of development in England and Wales. I am certainly not here to give a Pommy lecture to Australians about how you can learn from us."But as one education historian has written, '[Baker] then proceeded to deliver a lecture about how Australians could indeed learn from the mother country."[20]

The full Thatcher education agenda was laid out in great detail: testing, choice, competition, school autonomy, business plans, principal contracts and local budgets. The New South Wales (NSW) Education Minister, Terry Metherell, responded, 'I have made two visits to Britain and observed the Baker Revolution taking place.We can learn much from their vision and their passion for reform."[21] It is of little surprise that Metherell would seek to emulate Baker. The NSW head of government at the time, the NSW Premier Nick Greiner, was inclined to speak of NSW as a company, NSW Inc., rather than a state, referring to its citizens as shareholders.

Within months of taking office, the Greiner Government had appointed a management consultancy firm headed by Brian Scott to undertake a review of education in NSW. Scott's son soon became an adviser to the Minister. Neither father nor son had any experience in public education but this did not prevent them from publishing a report called *Schools Renewal: A Strategy to Revise Schools within the New South Wales State Education System*. But it was easy work as the strategy was essentially already being unleashed on British schools and borrowed heavily from Tory Party policy.

Scott's report was classic neo-liberalism; public schools ought to be managed more like private businesses. The Department of Education was characterised as an 'out of touch' bureaucracy and its head office in the centre of Sydney was destined to be sold. The staffing of schools was the first target. Thousands of teachers were dismissed, class sizes were increased, and cleaning services were privatised. Each school was to compete for enrolments based on a school plan that was to highlight its main selling points to the community. Competition and difference was encouraged; cooperation and notions of commonality discouraged. The language of teaching and learning became infused with managerial jargon. Schooling was to become a market place and not all were expected to survive. The 'self-managing school' was to be the model for the future.

In essence, the *Schools Renewal* report had very little to do with education. No school was renewed. It was a management report that went to school governance and structural changes. Financial management and staffing responsibility was to be devolved to the school level while at the same time responsibility for curriculum was to be more tightly controlled by the Minister. It was only the determination of the teachers who through their union campaigned against the agenda that spared students from the most extreme of the proposed changes.

An even more radical set of policies was introduced in 1993 by a Liberal Government in the state of Victoria headed by Premier Jeff Kennett. The policy was called Schools of the Future. Having learnt from the mistakes of his NSW counterparts who had rolled out the agenda over many months allowing for opposition to grow, Kennett moved swiftly. Once again he borrowed heavily from Thatcher's England. The devastation on the Victorian public education system was unprecedented in Australian history. Over 350 schools were closed across the state. More than 8000 teachers lost their jobs. $500 million was cut from the education budget.

As a former Liberal politician proclaimed, 'The Kennett Government reduced the size of the head office function and the central bureaucracy in the Department of Education to the bone.'[22]

Victoria became the most devolved school system in the country but with the lowest level of per capita funding of any state. Not only was public education affected. Public transport services were privatised with the loss of 16,000 jobs. Gas and electricity utilities, many health and community services, including ambulance services, and prisons were privatised.

But across Australia there have been other significant number of government policies introduced nationally and at the state level to restructure public education systems based on market driven ideology and 'new public management' theory. They have all been launched with accompanying glossy brochures and marketed with catchy titles. These include:

Directions for Education, Tasmania (1996)
Leading Schools, Queensland (1997)
Independent Public Schools, Western Australia (2009)
Empowering Local Schools, Australia (2010)
Local Schools, Local Decisions, New South Wales (2012)
Independent Public Schools, Queensland (2013)

The Western Australian (WA) experiment with the notion of 'independent public schools' had national significance at a national level after the election of the conservative Coalition Government in 2013. Its policy is to spread the model to public schools systems throughout Australia. It is essentially a self-managing school model. But the reality is that the WA Independent Public Schools model never had its origins in education theory. Rather it was the creation of the WA Government Economic Audit Committee's (EAC) report, 'Putting the Public First', once again borrowing heavily from conservative ideology such as 'Big Society'. The WA audit report unveiled massive changes to management structures across the entire WA public service, not just schools. [23]

The New Zealand Government's model, *Tomorrow's Schools*, was introduced in 1989 and has resulted in New Zealand schools operating in one of the most devolved systems in the world. Dr Cathie Wylie of the NZ Council Education Research has documented the consequences of this in her book Vital Connections.

At a national level, Australian Governments have had less influence than some other national governments because of the federal system. There have been sporadic attacks on curriculum from conservative politicians, and an increasing form of 'coercive federalism' due to the national governments control of financial grants to the state but it is in the area of testing and funding that the national government has more direct influence.

It has been the capacity of the national teachers' union, the Australian Education Union (AEU), to intervene effectively in these two policy areas that has interrupted the neo-liberal agenda.

A national testing agenda was developed, replacing state-based testing regimes, in 2008 called the National Assessment Program – Literacy and Numeracy (NAPLAN) for Years 3, 5, 7 and 9. In January of 2010, the then Labor Government developed a national website called My School. This website was to publish each school's NAPLAN test data. Immediately, a relatively benign testing agenda, compared to countries such as the USA and the UK, had become high stakes. Student assessment was to become an adult spectator sport.

The Australian Education Union responded by attempting to negotiate with the Federal Government for a set of protocols and protections to be developed around the use of the data to prevent the creation of 'league tables'. For months there was no breakthrough and the national union called for a ban on the NAPLAN tests due to be sat in May of 2010. This was supported unanimously by the AEU's federal executive representing all states and territories. The vast majority of principals are members of the AEU and many led their school communities in support of the union ban on NAPLAN.

Finally, the national government was forced to negotiate a set of protections that included technical changes to the website to make it difficult for media groups to harvest the test data in order to create 'league tables'. The tests went ahead but an entire generation was educated about the dangers of the misuse of test data.

The former schools funding regime has been largely discredited due to decades of determined campaigning by teacher unions in alliance with parents and sections of the community. This led to the Federal Labor Government, upon retaining office in 2007, to establish an inquiry into schools funding. A committee was established chaired by prominent Australian businessman, David Gonski. The panel's final report, *Review of Funding for Schooling*, was presented to the Government in late 2011. It has become known as the Gonski Review. The campaign to secure the full implementation of the Gonski recommendations is continuing. The campaign has generated huge support across the country. Social media, such as the www.igiveagonski.com.au website and Facebook page has been a critical factor in harnessing this support.

A warning: an approaching tsunami

Education has always been an area of public policy hotly contested. After all, it has been where the tensions between church and state have been, and are still, played out, where individual privilege keeps defending its territory from encroaching ideas of public good and where social conservatives have consistently attempted to intervene in the school curriculum. But the last three to four decades has seen a much more organised, coherent and well-funded campaign underpinned by the ideology of the market. It is this influence of neo-liberal ideology that is having the most dramatic effect on public education around the world as it is so much more than just a contest of ideas.

But there is no doubt that we are only at the beginning of the neo-liberal era. The next phase is the full privatisation agenda with the rise of 'edu-businesses' which are stalking public education in order to turn what historically has been a public good into private profit. Australian educator, Steve Dinham, sounds the warning likening the changes as akin to an approaching tsunami, often unnoticed before it is too late:

> "*A further international development impacting on Australia is the entry of 'big business' into education. There has always been a commercial aspect to education with providers of textbooks, resources and equipment but this is escalating almost exponentially. Publishers are now moving into large scale vertical integration whereby they have commercial involvement with curricula, teaching resources, teaching standards, teacher training, development and appraisal, and student assessment and testing; in effect gaining control of the entire education supply chain.*" [24]

A united teacher union movement, at home and across the globe, is now more important than at any time in our history.

Bibliography

Ansary, Tamin (2007) *Education as Risk: Fallout From a Flawed Report* (www.edutopia.org/landmark-education-report-nation-risk)

Bracey, Gerald W. (2004) *Setting the Record Straight: Responses to Misconceptions About Public Education in the U.S.* Heinemann

Davies, Nick (1999) *Schools in crisis, part 3: How Tory political coup bred educational disaster* The Guardian, 17 September 1999

Devereaux, Jenni (2013) *The Expansion of Free Schools in the UK* Australian Education Union Federal Conference Papers, February 2013

Dinham, Stephen (2014) *The Worst of Both Worlds: How the US and UK are Influencing Education in Australia* (Walter Neal Oration, Australian College of Educators, Perth)

Fabricant, Michael and Fine, Michelle (2012) *Charter Schools and the Corporate Makeover of Public Education* Teachers College Press

Fiala, Thomas J. and Owens, Deborah (2010) *Education Policy and 'Friedmanomics': Free Market Ideology and Its Impact on School Reform* Paper presented 23 April 2010 at the Midwest Political Science Association 68th Annual National Conference, Chicago, Illinois

Fitzgerald, Scott and Rainnie, Al (2011) *Putting the Public First? An examination of the implications of the 2009 EAC Report – Part Two: Independent Public Schools* Curtin Graduate School of Business

Fitzgerald, Denis (2011) *Teachers and Their Times: History and the Teachers Federation* UNSW Press

Gillard, Derek (2011) *Education in England: a brief history* www.educationengland.org.uk/history

Jones, Ken (2003) *Education in Britain: 1944 to the Present* Polity Press

Joseph, Keith (1976) *Monetarism Is Not Enough* www.margaretthatcher.org/document/110796

McCollow, John (2013) *Charter Schools and Marginalised Ethnic and Racial Groups – Implications for Australia?* Report to Australian Education Union Federal Conference, February 2013

Moll, Marita [ed] (2004) *Passing the Test: The False Promises of Standardized Testing* Canadian Centre for Policy Alternatives

Mortimore, Peter (2013) *Education Under Siege* Policy Press – University of Bristol

Mulheron, Maurie (2014) *If We Forget History* NSW Teachers Federation

Musset, Pauline (2012) *School Choice and Equity* OECD Working Paper No 66

National Commission on Excellence in Education (April 1983) *A Nation at Risk: The Imperative for Educational Reform* (U.S. Government Printing Office Washington)

NOUS Group (2011) *Schooling Challenges and Opportunities* www.deewr.gov.au

OECD (2013). *PISA 2012 Results: What Makes Schools Successful? Resources, Policies and Practices (Volume IV)*. Paris: OECD Publishing.

Ravitch, Diane (2013) *Reign of Error: The Hoax of the Privatisation Movement and the Danger to America's Public Schools* Alfred A. Knopf

Sahlberg, Pasi (2011) *Finnish Lessons: what can the world learn from educational change in Finland* Teachers College Press

Teese, Richard (2011) *From opportunity to outcomes. The changing role of public schooling in Australia and national funding arrangements*, Centre for Research on Education Systems, University of Melbourne

Verger, Antoni; Altinyelken, H K; Koning, M [eds] (2013) p1 *Global Managerial Education Reforms and Teachers Education* International Research Institute

Vinovskis, Maria (1999) *The Road to Charlottesville: The 1989 Education Summit* (A National Education Goals Panel NEGP Paper)

Weiner, Lois (2012) *The Future of Our Schools: Teachers, Unions and Social Justice* Haymarket Books

Whelan, James (2012) *Big Society and Australia: How the UK Government is dismantling the state and what it means for Australia* Centre for Policy Development

Wylie, Cathy (2012) *Vital Connections: Why we need more than self-managing schools* NZCER Press

Footnotes

1. Organisation for Economic Co-operation and Development (2013). *PISA 2012 Results: What Makes Schools Successful? Resources, Policies and Practices (Volume IV)*. Paris: OECD Publishing.
2. OECD PISA 2012 Results, Table IV3.17, p. 339
3. NOUS Group, *Schooling Challenges and Opportunities* August 2011, pp 20-21 http://www.deewr.gov.au/Schooling/ReviewofFunding/Documents/NousSchoolingChallengesandOpportunities.pdf
4. Musset, P, *School Choice and Equity*, OECD Working Paper No 66, 2012

5   Teese, R. (2011), *From opportunity to outcomes. The changing role of public schooling in Australia and national funding arrangements*, Centre for Research on Education Systems, University of Melbourne

6   Verger, Antoni; Altinyelken, H K; Koning, M [eds] (2013) p1 *Global Managerial Education Reforms and Teachers Education* International Research Institute

7   Kemp, David quoted in Dr James Whelan (May 2012) p 57, *Big Society and Australia -How the U.K. Government is dismantling the state and what it means for Australia*. Centre for Policy Development

8   *A Nation at Risk: The Imperative for Educational Reform* (April 1983) Washington DC, USA

9   Tamin Ansary *Education as Risk: Fallout From a Flawed Report* (www.edutopia.org/landmark-education-report-nation-risk)

10 Vinovskis, Maria (1999) *The Road to Charlottesville: The 1989 Education Summit* (A National Education Goals Panel NEGP Paper) p11

11 Larry Kuehn, p62, 'Leaning Between Conspiracy and Hegemony' in Marita Moll (2004) *Passing the Test: The False Promises of Standardized Testing* Canadian Centre for Policy Alternatives

12 Kjell Eide, p48 *30 Years Of Educational Collaboration In The O.E.C.D.* (Paper to International Planning and Management of Educational Development Conference, Mexico, 26-30 March 1990)

13 www.oecd.org/about/

14 Larry Kuehn p 65 *The New Right Agenda in Education* published in Education for Social Justice

15 Gillard, Derek (2011) *Education in England: a brief history* www.educationengland.org.uk/history

16 Joseph, Keith (1976) *Monetarism Is Not Enough* www.margaretthatcher.org/document/110796

17 Nick Davies (1999) *Schools in crisis, part 3: How Tory political coup bred educational disaster* The Guardian 17 September 1999

18 Jones, (2003) p 107 quoted in Gillard, Derek

19 Gillard

20 Fitzgerald, Denis p94 Teachers and Their Times: History and the Teachers Federation (2011) UNSW Press

21 Fitzgerald, Denis p95

22 Phil Honeywood, The World Today, ABC Radio 2 Feb 2000.

23 Fitzgerald, Scott and Rainnie, Al

24 Dinham, Stephen p11 The Worst of Both Worlds: How the US and UK are Influencing Education in Australia 2014

3 Teacher solidarity across borders is essential in response to the impact of neo-liberal globalization

Larry Kuehn

THE GLOBAL Education Reform Movement (GERM) is an illness infecting education systems globally. The source of the illness is, in its essence, abandoning education's role of creating and recreating social and cultural good and building social cohesion. In its place, education is seen primarily as preparing workers to compete in a global economy.

The mechanisms used to propagate GERM are at least three: testing, technology and corporate capitalism. Each of these three elements will be described in their separate impact, as well as how they come together. The International Solidarity Programme of the British Columbia Teachers' Federation (BCTF) will then be outlined as a key component of our response to GERM and the mechanisms used to propagate it.

Testing — and specifically the PISA exams drive education 'reform'

PISA is the acronym for the 'Programme for International Student Assessment." It is a project of the OECD, the Organization for Economic Cooperation and Development.

The PISA exam has become the most significant factor in influencing education policies around the globe, including in all three NAFTA countries (Canada, Mexico, USA). When new exam results are released in the form of league tables - lists giving a single number average result - the rankings get extensive publicity, and often wrong conclusions.

I was in the U.S. when the results from the most recent PISA math tests were announced. The media was full of claims that the schools are a disaster and the future of the American economy is threatened.

In Mexico, which came near the bottom of the rankings, those PISA results were used as a rationale for the education reforms that abandon long-held societal goals and undermine the rights of teachers.

Canada, in contrast, came out near the top in the PISA rankings. Despite that, we still heard the results as a reason for changing our system of education. The claim was that we might not maintain such a high position if we don't change. This despite no one having a crystal ball to predict the future economy, nor any research showing a different approach would produce a better result for learning - or for economic competitiveness.

Regardless of results, PISA tests are used by politicians and bureaucrats to justify changes to education policy - to adopt the Global Education Reform Movement.

The tests are now given in more than 60 countries and many more have joined the 2015 round. In effect, the OECD through PISA has become the de facto governor of education directions globally.

Naomi Klein describes the process that is used to create a climate for neo-liberal change as the "Shock Doctrine." Low scores provide an opportunity to promote some action already planned, claiming the actions answer a problem.[1]

The immediate response to low results is to blame the teachers. Most of the prescriptions for improving results attack existing structures and call for discipline of teachers through regulations. Mexico, for example, has used the results to demand tests of the teachers.

Seldom does any politician actually read the more detailed reports on PISA. One of those PISA reports[2] points out that the biggest factor in the difference in results is not teachers, but poverty. The social conditions in which students live has a major impact. Canada does better than the U.S. - it also has lower levels of child poverty. The US and Canada do better than Mexico, which has a much larger rate of child poverty.

Clearly poverty is not the only factor - teachers and schools do have an impact, but less than the out of school factors.

Canada also has more equality in funding education than does the U.S., meaning that the resources available to support students in school are more equal, regardless of student socio-economic status. A study of this aspect of the PISA results for Canada identified the lower gap between top and bottom social status as a factor in producing higher average results.[3]

The point about poverty is effectively made in an infographic that shows the impact of poverty on PISA results both within the U.S. and in international comparisons. I found it on the Facebook feed from the "Bad Ass Teachers" a Facebook group any teacher should follow who feels the need to resist the impact of the Global Education Reform Movement.[4]

If the OECD knows that poverty is the most significant factor in the range of scores on PISA, why are governments who claim to be concerned about education not moving to eliminate poverty and equalize education funding? Because it is easier and cheaper for governments to blame the teachers and bring in programs to "fix" those teachers.

The World Bank and the International Monetary Fund

Before PISA, the World Bank and the International Monetary Fund were the most influential institutions with an impact on education in less developed or "emerging" economies. Mostly they have focused on structural issues and teacher "accountability."

● They promote Charter Schools.
● They recommend that countries without universal education get more of the world's children into primary education but without providing funds for reasonable class sizes or professional levels of pay.
● They call for decentralization in responsibility for funding education, but centralizing the control of content and teachers.

Now one of their reports[5] calls for videotaping of teachers and coding their teaching against a rubric to see whether they should get a bonus or be fired. This is the Gates Foundation techno-solution - sometimes characterized as "firing the way to Finland." The theory is that by firing the least effective teachers every year, the quality of teachers will be as good as that in Finland.

When we look at data out of context:

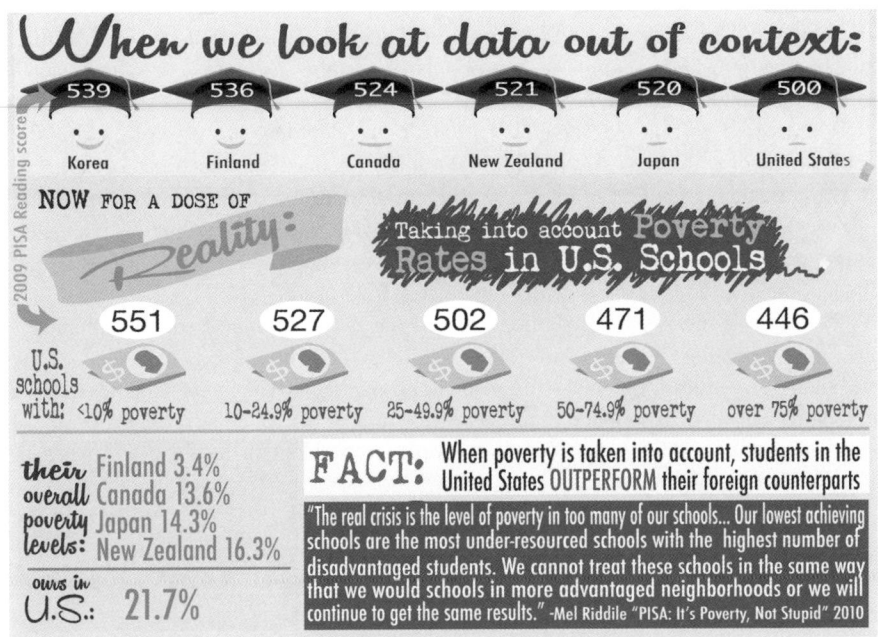

539	536	524	521	520	500
Korea	Finland	Canada	New Zealand	Japan	United States

2009 PISA Reading score

NOW FOR A DOSE OF Reality: Taking into account Poverty Rates in U.S. Schools

551	527	502	471	446
U.S. schools with: <10% poverty	10-24.9% poverty	25-49.9% poverty	50-74.9% poverty	over 75% poverty

their Finland 3.4%
overall Canada 13.6%
poverty Japan 14.3%
levels: New Zealand 16.3%
ours in
U.S.: 21.7%

FACT: When poverty is taken into account, students in the United States OUTPERFORM their foreign counterparts

"The real crisis is the level of poverty in too many of our schools... Our lowest achieving schools are the most under-resourced schools with the highest number of disadvantaged students. We cannot treat these schools in the same way that we would schools in more advantaged neighborhoods or we will continue to get the same results." -Mel Riddile "PISA: It's Poverty, Not Stupid" 2010

reference article: http://nasspblogs.org/principaldifference/2010/12/pisa_its_poverty_not_stupid_1.html

The World Bank and IMF join in blaming the teacher and demanding that teachers be fixed rather than fixing the social conditions of the children.

These international institutions still have a lot of power, particularly in less developed countries, but the OECD has more and growing impact on global education policies.

A second major influence on education globally is information and communications technologies

The spread of new ICTs has been rapid and ubiquitous. It has created a new environment for our children - one whose impact is not well understood. In fact, it is hard to imagine how it can be understood when its shape and dimension changes so rapidly. In this environment, we see many schemes and ideas for how technology could change education. Many of these are promoted as answering the enduring questions of education - for what purpose, how, and whose interests are served. As with the PISA results, policy-makers are presented with claims that particular technologies will prepare children to succeed in the global economy.

This growth in technology comes at a time that corporate capital has identified public education as the last great global money pot to tap into by privatization.

One Laptop Per Child has sold more than two million laptops in Latin America. Millions of tablets have been purchased as well. The rationale is always to prepare the country for competition in the global economy.

All sorts of positive claims are made for the adoption of technology for education - many are at the stage that the 'Gartner Hype Cycle' [6] labels 'peak of inflated expectations."Three particular directions fit into the inflated expectations stage: testing, adaptive learning and data mining. The promise is that they will turn your school system in a 21st century winner in the global race

Here as well, testing sets the global education agenda. One of the most high profile applications of technology in the U.S. is the billion dollar iPad fiasco in Los Angeles. Not only was there conflict of interest in the purchase of the iPads, but the curriculum resources added were from the Pearson corporation and intended to prepare students for the Pearson-developed Common Core tests. A survey of teachers whose classes did get iPads indicated the Pearson resources were very little used.

The intent of this mass distribution of iPads was not to produce creative exploration, the implicit promise. Rather, it was to have students ready for tests, a centrepiece of the Common Core. Indeed, the next PISA exam to be given in 2015 is to be computer-based . Students who have experience in online testing may well have an advantage over those who have not. This will again provide an opportunity to blame the teacher for things over which they have little control.

"Adaptive learning" is the next 'big thing." In essence, it is an attempt to make education more "efficient"by automating aspects of teaching. It leads a student through some aspect of learning, adapting the questions it asks and material it supplies to student responses.

Ironically, this approach is referred to as 'personalization." One concept of personalization could be a vision of technology as a platform of creative activity activity that is not pre-determined, but an expression of student creativity. But adaptive learning is not that kind of personalization. Rather, it is pre-determined what direction the student is to take and what can be varied is the time it takes to develop the understanding or skill to reach that pre-determined objective.

Then there is Big Data and data mining, another element to the 'next big thing." Audrey Watters in an article called 'Student Data is the New Oil"describes the way that student data becomes a minable resource.

If all the data points created by a student, and by students collectively, can be captured, then algorithms can be used to mine all this data. Massive databases of student information are being developed, supposedly to be able to find the route that a student should take. Every keystroke captured, every website visited tracked, every conversation with friends monitored - and metadata collected about all this online activity.

Metadata - this is something we have learned about through the revelations of Edward Snowden about how much data we are producing - and how little we realize that we are all the subject of surveillance. And surveillance can be turned into profits. When school systems build huge databases, the potential and temptation is there to share data with marketers. The InBloom school data project seems to have been killed when parents found out how their children's data would be marketed, but don't imagine that is the last attempt to do this.

Tests and data link to a third element of the Global Education Reform Movement: Corporate capital attempts to take over public education

Many of the themes developed previously come together when looking at the role of corporate capital in a possible takeover of education globally.

It may seem like a conspiracy theory to talk about this. But you need look no further than one company that is positioning itself to develop a near-monopoly of the digital in education: the Pearson corporation.

Pearson describes itself as the "global learning company." It, like other major textbook publishers, faces the challenge of a new revenue stream since print textbooks are in rapid decline. Pearson's policy now is that it is only-digital. It is preparing itself to move out from making most of its fortune primarily in the most developed countries and focusing on "emerging markets," many of these being in Latin America.

Pearson has moved into all these areas: Curriculum and standards, including the Common Core Curriculum; online K-12 courses; digital learning resources; standardized tests; test preparation; identifying test cheaters; operating private schools in the developing world, as well as Charter schools; student information systems; alternative high school certification; teacher licensing tests; teacher training and certification programs.

And Pearson has the contract with the OECD to run the next round of PISA exams. It then gives recommendations for education reform based on the tests that it creates. Diane Ravich correctly says "The corporation is acting as a quasi-government agency in several instances, but it is not a quasi-government agency: it is a business that sells products and services."[7]

Imagine how large a database it is developing - and think about who owns that information, even if it is stripped of its link to an individual. Teachers in New York have been in a conflict with Pearson. It prohibits teachers from looking at the questions in tests that it has developed for the new Common Core. It wants to be able to reuse the tests in other "markets," so it wants full control over all the data. This data is no longer owned by the student or the teacher, or even the school board that pays Pearson to give the tests. It all becomes part of a rapidly growing set of data that Pearson can use to develop products to sell back to the people who create the data - and whose lives and identities are reflected in it.

So back to our opening question. How do the OECD's PISA exams, information and communications technology and corporate capital all come together in ways that are a threat to public control of education?

The audit and accountability culture of the GERM makes it ever more possible to take education out of the hands of those who create it and should own it - teachers, students and the public. Instead we are seeing it turned into an internationally tradable commodity.

Collectively we need to understand the nature of this globalization. And we need to work together to develop strategies that interrupt and challenge the culture of GERM.

International solidarity is key to this which is why the BCTF International Solidarity Programme is an important component of our response to GERM.

International solidarity, not charity

Teachers are everywhere, and more than 30 million belong to unions. And education can be an agent for social justice - or not.

Free, quality public education opens opportunity for many, in contrast to systems that have private, quality education for an elite, and poor public schools - or none - for the rest.

This opens for us a unique opportunity to challenge GERM as a component of international solidarity, both in a practical sense and on a cultural and ideological level.

Samora Machel, the first president of an independent Mozambique, captured the essence of our understanding of the meaning of solidarity:

'International solidarity is not an act of charity. It is an act of unity between allies fighting on different terrains toward the same objectives. The foremost of these objectives is to aid the development of humanity to the highest level possible."

The strategic focus of the BC Teachers' Federation's (BCTF) International Solidarity Program and Fund is to support teacher unions as they put the ideals of public education into practice. This includes improving the working conditions of teachers and the learning conditions of students, as well as promoting accessible and quality public schools.

Raising funds to build schools, provide school supplies, and assist individual teachers seems commendable. However, for sustainable action for quality public education, effective teacher unions have a key role, pressing governments to provide resources on an ongoing basis. It is in this context that the BCTF has for more than three decades worked in partnership with teacher unions in Latin America and in Southern Africa.

The internationalism of the BCTF is almost as old as the union itself. The first BCTF General Secretary, Harry Charlesworth, participated in the creation of an international education organization in 1923, only a few years after the formation of the BCTF.

The current version of international solidarity at the BCTF has been in place for more than 30 years, with the commitment of a portion of members' dues on an ongoing basis, and the creation of an International Solidarity Committee.

An initial focus of the work in Latin America from the mid-1980s and still continuing now is on gender issues, particularly providing financial support for the development of programs to promote the engagement of women in their unions. Women are large majorities of teachers and any union that does not have a central place for women is weaker than it should be. These programs developed by women teachers have moved into challenging the content of education and top-down curriculum with non-sexist pedagogy.

A second major stream of the work has been to challenge neo-liberal policies—GERM is the application of these policies in education. The initial focus of this work was trade agreements and the negative impact they would have on public education. This work of the BCTF began with participating in the creation of the Tri-national Coalition in Defense of Public Education in response to NAFTA (North American Free Trade Agreement). The BCTF played a role in the formation of the Tri-national and has been a committed partner in its ongoing operation, including providing funding for activities for the Mexican Section of the Tri-national and the holding of conferences every second year, alternating among Canada, Mexico and the US.

When NAFTA came into force in 1994, it was the first multi-national trade agreement to incorporate trade in services. Previously trade agreements had been about goods, but not services. Thinking about education as an internationally tradable product was a significant shift from education seen primarily as a social-cultural element in the context of a nation. Seeing education as a tradable commodity leads logically to the three themes identified earlier as elements of GERM: standardized testing for cross-national comparisons and defining what is valued in education, which became the PISA exam; the application of information technology required to handle the level of information required for these cross-national comparisons; and the role of trans-national corporations hoping to sell as a commodity all aspects of education, with Pearson being the leading example of the corporate role.

In the late 1990s, the Clinton administration set an objective of developing a Free Trade Area of the Americas, aiming essentially to expand NAFTA to cover all the Americas. Growing out of the Tri-national Coalition experience, the BCTF funded a conference in Quito, Ecuador in 1999 that developed into the IDEA Network (Initiative for Democratic Education in the Americas, Red-SEPA in the Spanish version of the name). It brought together people from around the Americas, from student and community groups, as well as teacher unions.

The work of both the Tri-national Coalition and the IDEA Network has expanded well beyond the specific focus on opposing trade agreements. It should not be forgotten, thought, that many transnational trade agreements continue to be negotiated, including the Transatlantic Trade and Investment Partnership (TTIP) and the Comprehensive Economic and Trade Agreement (CETA). All of these are designed to privilege corporate interests by making all aspects of human activity into tradable commodities and limiting the ability of the state to adopt laws or policies that limit the ability of corporations to make profits.

Most of the activities of the Tri-national and the IDEA Network could be described as research and communications related to the elements of GERM, and further expressions and actions of solidarity for those involved in struggles in support of public education in the local and global contexts. In addition to seminars and conferences and research, the IDEA Network maintains a website and publishes in Spanish and English an online and hard copy publication called Intercambio [http://idea-network.ca/category/intercambio-magazine].

Challenging the standardized testing mania and the impact of PISA was addressed in a joint seminar. The work from that seminar was widely circulated on dvd, particularly in Latin America, providing teacher unions with resources for critical examination of policies on standardized testing. Particularly since several countries in Latin America have joined the PISA test process, critical work has been carried out in opposing this external definition of national education policies.

Issues related to the impact of technology have been an important part of the work of the IDEA Network, as well. A multi-country seminar looked particularly at the political economy of education technology. Technology is promoted almost everywhere as key to future success of a country in the global economy. The millions of computers supplied by the One Laptop per Child program, along with masses of netbooks and tablets bought by governments, have appeared in schools with little actual take-up in educational uses.

Teachers have concerns about expectations placed on them by techo-enthusiast ministries which offer little or no training for teachers on effective use. In fact, the lack of training reflects a lack of any good research or useful ideas about appropriate pedagogy. Wasted resources are taken away from creating better classroom conditions.

The IDEA Network held a seminar on education technology in Mexico City that contributed to an issue of *Intercambio* [http://idea-network.ca/wp-content/uploads/2014/09/INTERCAMBIO-6-Eng-WEB.pdf], providing critical perspectives on a number of areas, including online learning, data analytics, pedagogy, research on One Laptop per Child, and teachers' working conditions in online learning. Following that, several of the teacher unions in Central America created a project to carry out discussions on these issues in their countries, and are producing their own research on a regional basis, working to develop sound union policies about technology issues. FECODE, the teachers' union in Colombia and UNE, the union in Ecuador, organized workshops in several communities in both countries where I presented an analysis of the political economy of technology in education.

A current focus of the IDEA Network is the troubled state of teacher employee benefits. In line with neo-liberal policies everywhere, pensions and other benefits are under attack. In some cases, governments have taken control of teacher pension funds; in others, retirement ages are being raised and benefits being reduced. The IDEA Network is bringing together teacher union activists from several countries who can share experiences, analysis and ideas for action.

Forces promoting GERM have lots of international connections and shared strategies for pushing their reform movement. It is essential that the same be available for those who support the ideals and practice of democratic public education. Bringing together activists from a range of countries focused on particular aspects of the GERM program helps us all to see the international dimensions of what is happening in our own countries. This knowledge is a contribution to a deep sense of solidarity, a key intention of the BCTF International Solidarity Program.

Footnotes

1 Klein, Naomi. (2007). *The Shock Doctrine: The rise of disaster capitalism.*
2 OECD (2010). PISA 2009 Results: Executive Summary. Downloaded from http://www.oecd.org/pisa/pisaproducts/46619703.pdf
3 OECD (2013). PISA 2012 Results: *Excellence Through Equity: Giving Every Student the Chance to Succeed*, Volume 2. Downloaded from http://dx.doi.org/10.1787/9789264201132-en
4 Christinemccartney
5 Strauss, Valerie. 'Bill Gates $5 billion plan to videotape America's teachers."*Washington Post*, May, May 10, 2013.

6 'Garner Hype Cycle." http://www.gartner.com/technology/research/methodologies/hype-cycle.jsp
7 'Pearson a digital hydra in education." http://digicritic.blogspot.ca/2014/02/pearson-digital-hydra-in-education.html

Other references:

Meyer, H-D and Benavot, A., eds. (2013). PISA, Power and Policy: the emergence of global educational governance. (Oxford, U.K.: Symposium Books)

Watters, A. (2013). "Student Data is the New Oil: MOOCs, Metaphor, and Money." Downloaded May 5, 2014 from http://hackeducation.com/2013/10/17/student-data-is-the-new-oil/

4 Lessons from the Global South

Lars Dahlström and Brook Lemma

Towards the end of the twentieth century a sickness struck the world. Not everyone died, but all suffered from it. The virus which caused the epidemic was called the "liberal virus". (Amin, 2004)

THIS NARRATIVE is based on educational interventions in the global South. It tells a story of hegemonic influences and attempts of counter-hegemonic resistance and solidarity.

The omnipresence of the global reform agenda is sometimes difficult to recognize as local conditions transform its appearance even though the reform agenda itself follows the same idea of "one size fits all". We can see the patterns of assaults more clearly if we use an historical perspective and look at how it has been played out locally in different places. The machinery of the global reform agenda is maintained by many global forces of which the PISA hit lists in the North and the EFA reform agenda in the South, both lubricated by the oil of new public management, are amongst the most influential, together with straightforward privatisations.

Education for All (EFA) was introduced in the global South as an UNESCO flagship in 1990 for countries in the South who were dependent on external financial support to the educational sector. The EFA reforms were further strengthened through the Millennium Goals (MG) in 2000 and both systems are continuously monitored in relation to the goals that are supposed to be met by 2015. The 'international development community' is at the moment busy devising the next generation of international development goals through a post-2015 development process, while the official promises of EFA and MG are left behind. Meanwhile, the unofficial agenda to install a western individualised and neoliberal market ideology is strongly becoming the hegemonic paradigm also in the global South.

Another group of players, the venture capitalists and philanthropic networks based on neoliberal business policies, have entered the educational arena in support of the westernization and marketization of education. These neoliberal networks induce new policy aspects as 'silver bullet' solutions following market-based solutions to social problems.

However, systems created by humans are never perfect and we will always find cracks where alternatives can grow even in the midst of the h

egemonic influences. Counter-hegemonic alternatives will sustain at least as individual and collective engravings that will influence local practices as well as future actions and positioning, even when not sustained at systemic levels.

National contexts and neo-liberal assaults

Here we will make an overview of the situations in four African countries Botswana, Namibia, South Africa and Ethiopia.

Botswana – not only a landlocked country

One of us came to Botswana as a volunteer in the beginning of 1980s to work in an international in-service education project with a British leadership. The duty was to support the educational development at village primary schools together with a local Education Officer. The subtitle of the project was "a different sort of thing" which was a sign of acceptance of the local situation and local demands. The work developed into a support to local language learning (Setswana) and reading material based on local situation as a contrast to the official 'Betty and David" readers copied from England. We introduced a Language Experience Approach based on village life and produced readers from local experiences and traditional stories told by teachers. The readers were printed and distributed to schools.

After some time all Education Officers including the volunteers in this project were called to a workshop in the capital Gaborone. We were going to be briefed and introduced to a new national project called the Primary Education Improvement Project (PEIP). PEIP was financed by the World Bank (WB) and staffed by the United States Agency for International Development (USAID) and we were instructed that all support activities to teachers and schools in the country should follow the PEIP agenda as a matter of efficiency in respect to learning outcomes. 'Learner-centred education' was the catchword of this agenda as has been the case in the international development community up until today. This tradition of learner-centred education is based on a highly individualized perspective that can be linked back to Rousseau and the European enlightenment in mid-1700s as well as to the work of Piaget in mid-1900s. This tradition has therefore also a highly westernized bias even beyond its pedagogical aspects as a political artefactfor modernisation necessary in pluralistic and liberal capitalist societies. Learner-centred education became one of the tools to infuse ways of thinking and practices supportive to the western agenda.

The marginalisation of the pedagogical aims became obvious when we were made aware of the strategy to implement learner-centred education. It followed what was called a 'cascade model' as a supposed effective way to spread learner-centred education as pedagogy but also as a western artefact. The concept of learner-centred education became known by every teacher in the country as a way to give the learners more power in the learning process. In many classrooms this meant less teaching and teacher support and more laissez-faire and educational games. We learnt that the cascade model was an effective way to water down educative processes and to strengthen socio-political messages of modern schooling forwarding individualisation and marketization.

Namibia – The struggle between common sense and good sense

Namibia got its independence in 1990 after more than 25 years of liberation struggle against the illegal South African occupation. The liberation struggle was led by South West Africa People's Organisation (SWAPO) that after independence took over the political leadership in Namibia. Before independence one of us worked together with SWAPO in a refugee camp in Angola to educate the Namibian teachers who worked at the education centre in the camp. This teacher education followed a student-centred approach but different from the one applied in Botswana by PEIP. This alternative approach followed the traditions of Paulo Freire and Celestin Freinet as an empowering educative and political process and a pedagogy that related personal growth to situated learning and developed skills and knowledge through critical inquiry also beyond educational settings.

When independence came, we were asked to assist in the national reform of teacher education at the four colleges in Namibia. This was a complex field to work in, mainly because of the inherited dispositioning of people from the apartheid policies that had been exported to Namibia from South Africa. There was one teacher education college in Windhoek for white students and three colleges in the northern parts of the country for black students. The college for white students was considered to be a place of excellence, at least according to the apartheid thinking, while the northern colleges were considered more or less as overrated secondary schools. And all were instructed to apply the apartheid version of positivism and behaviourism called 'fundamental pedagogic' and its related 'bantu education' as a good enough model for black students.

With independence Namibia aimed at a new teacher education system for all that could break with the previous dispensation. It took many years to implement the new Basic Education Teachers' Diploma (BETD) as it was developed through a participatory process at the same time as a new National Institute for Educational Development (NIED) was established as a professional wing of the Ministry of Education. Teacher education was also intentionally not led by the newly established University of Namibia (UNAM). The reason was that its faculty of education was considered to be too conservative for the task of establishing something new. The BETD programme started in 1993 and replaced all previous programmes at the four colleges (all of which were ethnically oriented or ad-hoc interim courses controlled by the previous dispensation). The BETD was fully implemented in 1998 after two rounds of continuous development and evaluations of the three year programme.

The BETD programme was different from many other teacher education programmes in the way it was built up and organised also from an international perspective. It is worth noting that the Minister of Education in Namibia did not allow the World Bank to get involved in teacher education, even though it tried many times to get access to and redirect the development process during the first years after independence until it left the scene only to come back twenty years later.

In short, the characteristics of the BETD programme was that all students got the same kind of Diploma and the same salary no matter if their specialisation was in the lower primary, upper primary, or the junior secondary phases. The three years of teacher education were strongly connected to school based studies as well as a critical practitioner inquiry theme integrated with a subject combining pedagogy and methodology called Education Theory and Practice with links to other subject studies. Each college was also supported to develop an Educational Production Unit with printing and library facilities through which studies carried out by both teacher students and teacher educators could be printed and shared as an ambition to develop a new national knowledge base of education for the country.

The BETD programme became appreciated by many international researchers and teacher educators and even in comparative studies carried out with financial support from organisations that were sceptical of the critical educational philosophy behind the programme, such as the USAID and WB. However, on the ground in Namibia the programme received a lot of criticism and negative publicity from people who felt that they had lost their social status as skills built up under the apartheid era were marginalised. Calls for reform became stronger and stronger until the World Bank was allowed back both as a financial and monitoring partner. This altered the situation for teacher education fundamentally as the BETD programme was phased out from 2011 and replaced with traditional teacher education programmes delivered by UNAM. Furthermore, the independent colleges of education become satellite campuses of UNAM and students who previously received a grant from the government to cover the costs for their studies were forced to pay high university fees. The university fees became a deterring factor for poor students and created a sudden drop in student applications and a national problem to educate teachers, especially for the lower grades in primary education. The 'positive' side of this development was that all teacher educators became university lecturers and the few students who managed to finish the new B.Ed. degree programmes came out as the financial winners with higher salaries, supported by the teacher unions in Namibia. At the same time this accelerated the inequalities in the Namibian society and poor students who wanted a professional certification were left in the hands of private institutions that mushroomed after independence with sometimes doubtful promises.

South Africans betrayed –still amongst 'the poors'

Many who supported the liberation struggle for a better South Africa believed that a new education system would make a difference from 1994 when all South Africans for the first time went to the polls to vote against the racist apartheid regime. Twenty years have gone since the promises from the liberation struggle were going to become reality in South Africa.

Slavoj Zizek, an international acknowledged scholar wrote the following in the South African newspaper *Mail & Guardian*, when he got the message about Mandela's death in the beginning of December 2013.

People remember the old African National Congress that promised not only the end of apartheid, but also more social justice, even a kind of socialism. The miserable life of the poor majority broadly remains the same as under apartheid. The main change is that the old white ruling class is joined by the new black elite. If we want to remain faithful to Mandela's legacy, we should focus on the unfulfilled promises his leadership gave rise to.

Zizek continued and asked:

how to push things further after the first enthusiastic stage is over, how to make the next step without succumbing to the catastrophe of the totalitarian temptation – in short, how to move further from Mandela without becoming Mugabe?

So what went wrong in South Africa after 1994 in relation to education? Firstly, we must acknowledge that it was necessary to get rid of the parallel systems of education assigned to the racial groups in the society. Therefore, all schools had to allow all South African children their right to study irrespective of their social and racial background. The racial multiplication of universities, colleges, and other tertiary institutions were streamlined into one system for all. In addition to these administrative changes there was also an attempt to change the content of education through a curriculum reform.

Curriculum content had for long been a problem in South Africa. We remember the school strikes that became a strong political force from mid 1970s. Many serious educators were concerned about the state of education in South Africa even before 1994. For example, a national interim group of educators organized themselves in the beginning of 1990s to prepare for a different educational system in a South Africa free from apartheid and Bantu education. However, this South African group was more or less side-lined and overrun by an imported policy called Outcomes-Based Education (OBE).

OBE was initially introduced as a policy for the training of workshop managers under the support from the Congress of South African Trade Unions (COSATU) a strong ally to the ANC. Later on OBE was transferred to the national education system as a policy for curriculum development and systemic management.

The OBE originated from the USA where it was forcefully criticised but had been exported to Australia and further exported from there to South Africa. OBE had sometimes been given different names like mastery education, performance-based education, and at other times also framed as student-centred education. The basis of OBE was that the outcome of education was decided in advance in measurable terms. Almost like a modernised rebirth of the infamous fundamental pedagogics. Educational goals were formulated in a list of more than 70 general behavioural terms in the national curriculum called Curriculum 2005 that the teachers had to transform into operational and measurable behaviour amongst their students.

Today, when the failure of OBE is obvious and taken out from the curriculum, every responsible institution denies that they ever supported the OBE. The most obvious effect of the failure of OBE is the low pass rates of Grade 12 examinations, even though the government at times has affected the results by manipulating what counts as a pass. However the South African scholar Jonathan Jansen points to the not-so-obvious damaging costs of OBE. Jansen reminds us of the hundreds of millions of South African Rand that were spent to implement OBE, the costs of the lost opportunities that could have been taken since 1994, the motivational costs of teachers, parents, and students who were advised by the authorities and their administrators to support the OBE, the combined legacy costs of both the apartheid and the OBE systems that will continue to influence educational thinking and practices, the societal costs connected to the failure of the OBE system to produce people who can become productive members of an inclusive society, and most seriously the human costs for the disadvantaged who were exposed to an OBE system that turned already fragile learning environments to worse and forced many to leave the school system. Once more South Africa has to rethink its educational system and find a way to an educative upbringing of her disadvantaged people.

Ethiopia – how to bypass the teachers

Education reforms have for long been part of the development agenda in the Federal Democratic Republic of Ethiopia not least when new regimes have entered power positions.

When the government of the Federal Democratic Republic of Ethiopia (FDRE) came to power in 1991 a policy change was established, one of the main features of which was ethnic languages as the medium of instruction for primary education – corresponding to an Ethiopia that was changed to a combination of federal states with ethnic groups having language differences. The FDRE government also found the previous education system inadequate and the latest national reform within teacher education was initiated in 2003 under the label Teacher Education System Overhaul (TESO), including a call for student-centred methods in all government schools and universities.

TESO also introduced other international trends following neoliberal influences such as the shrinking of teacher education programmes of five years (including a year for practical teaching practice) to three years of intensive academic work only, national control of standardised identical curricula in all teacher education colleges and universities (with obvious variations in inputs and teacher quality and numbers), and the reduction of new study areas into technical packages for specific purposes. In addition to this, TESO introduced the most awkward example of student centred education, the 'plasma teachers'. An official government report to an UNESCO Conference in 2004, describes the introduction of this ICT technology as a way to strengthen the expansion of quality education. It was started at secondary level (grades 9 -12) to be followed at primary and ultimately all levels of education in the country. It included the production of educational TV programmes, installation of satellite receivers and plasma display panels in secondary schools and a national transmission system. Schools without electricity also got a generator and teachers and school managers were trained to use these devices.

This was the official picture of what was expected to happen in secondary classrooms in Ethiopia to enhance quality. How did this solution work out?

Students were doomed to watch lessons in natural sciences, mathematics, civics, ethical education, and English during four years of schooling presented on an uncommunicative plasma screen that continued to teach the lesson as planned even when students did not understand. It became a quick fix for modernization as young Ethiopians soon learnt to become modern by sleeping in front of the TV screen. Furthermore, the programmes were produced in South Africa by the most successful marketing university on the African continent, University of South Africa (UNISA), with the consequence that neither the South African English accent nor some of the social references in programmes were contextually accurate for secondary students in rural Ethiopia.

The plasma teachers became an enduring pain to students since its introduction as very little help was offered to students during or after the plasma teacher's performance. There was no time for the teacher in the classroom to carry out follow-up activities, because the next lesson started after the teacher had locked the case where the plasma screen was kept and it had been unlocked by another teacher in time for the next lesson to start on schedule according to the national time plan. There were instances when teachers were totally absent from school, such as going to a meeting called by the ministry of Education, and student leaders were operating the plasma television, as experienced at Alemaya high school.

Through this system, teachers were reduced to caretakers of plasma screens as their educational role in relation to the students was diminished significantly. Teachers did not even dare to disturb the plasma lesson as tests and examinations strictly followed the plasma script and no teacher wanted to be blamed for hindering students' learning. It was even said that the introduction of the plasma screens as a replacement for ordinary teachers was a way to stop teachers from demanding living salaries.

Frustrated educational administrators might have seen the plasma teachers as the salvation for education as it could bypass the troublesome middle-persons, the teachers, and establish a direct link to the students. They would thereby wrongly believe that education could be fixed by managerial systems and efficiency. Furthermore, if all students got the identical lessons, education became 'democratic and student centred' as there was no disturbing factor between the message and the student! However, analyses carried out through classroom observations showed that the plasma teachers replaced education as a social activity with information that a minority of students were able to transform to an acceptable grade in the examination. Very little quality education was involved. Plasma teachers were allowed to take centre stage and to bypass the teachers and reduce them to plasma gatekeepers.

In the middle of this educational swindle, we were asked by a Director of a UNESCO Institute in Addis Ababa, whether we could develop a Master course for teacher educators in Ethiopia following the Critical Practitioner Inquiry approach that we had developed in Namibia. This was carried out for a group of university lecturers working within teacher education. The group represented six different universities in the country and at present there are plans to develop this Master course even further to a PhD programme at least at one of these universities. There are always room for alternatives even in the most unexpected situations.

The latest information from Ethiopia is that the plasma reform at secondary level did not work out as expected! As a result of this expensive experiment many students have been robbed of their education, teachers of their pride, and the nation of its taxation money. The plasma screens have now a different purpose as the plasma teachers are replaced by propaganda officers of the political party in power, at least where the screens are still functioning.

Union responses and lessons learnt

The countries that are represented in this text have different histories of union activism and their role in society.

Botswana is an exception from most of the other countries in southern Africa as a country that did not need a liberation struggle to gain its independence. As a Protectorate under the British it was considered more or less as a waste land until the discovery of diamonds after independence in 1966. Two years ago the Botswana Teachers Union won a court case against the government. The government tried to prevent teachers from going on strike, according to Education International, who also opposed the repressive attitude of the Botswana government. The Botswana Democratic Party has governed the country since independence with a rather conservative policy supportive to business rather than workers' interests. Botswana has all along not only been a landlocked country but also driven by policies locked into conservative ideologies with strong ethnic roots and weak political oppositions.

The liberation struggle in Namibia and South Africa created a post-independence legacy where teachers' unions have close links to the present governments established by the previous liberation movements. This relationship has also a tendency of acceptance amongst the unions when globalised forces introduce their marketisation measures approved by the governments. The power of the unions will be further weakened if attempts to take away their striking rights are successful. These attempts are based on the claim that students' rights to education are affected negatively by striking teachers, as debated in South Africa.

The Ethiopian situation for students, teachers and teachers' unions is rather harsh. There are problems with low teacher salaries at all levels and harsh treatments of protesting students in addition to the attempt to rob teachers of their professional power through devises like the 'plasma teachers'.

All in all the space for critical actions on educational issues and teachers' work is very narrow in the countries covered in this overview. This is primarily due to the overwhelming pressure exerted by global capital both directly and via international financial institutions, a pressure which impacts on all governments, even those progressive governments which have grown out of national liberation movements.

However, it is possible to develop critical thoughts and practices that can alter the status quo and bring back resistance and solidarity to the mainstream, if the available degrees of freedom are strategically identified and used for counter-hegemonic activities. The key to this lies in the tensions experienced by both governments and unions between the pressure exerted by global capital and the pressure from their own people and their democratic aspirations.

As has been shown by the examples in this paper, these tensions can open up the spaces within which progressive educational alternatives can flourish. It is the exploitation of these tensions which provide the best opportunities to challenge the hegemony of neoliberalism in education.

References and further reading:

Amin, Samir (2004) *The Liberal Virus, Permanent War and the Americanization of the World.* New York: Monthly Review Press

Ball, Stephen J. (2012) *Global Education INC. New Policy Networks and the Neo-Liberal Imaginary.* London: Rutledge

Connell, Raewyn (2007) *Southern Theory.* Cambridge: Polity Press.

Dahlström, Lars (2002) *Post-apartheid teacher education reform in Namibia, The struggle between common sense and good sense.* Department of Education, Umeå University

Dahlström, Lars & Lemma, Brook (2008) Critical perspectives on teacher education in neo-liberal times: Experiences from Ethiopia and Namibia. *Southern African Review of Education*, Volume 14, Numbers 1-2. 29-42

Desai, Ashwin (2002) *We are the poors, community struggles in post-apartheid South* Africa. New York: Monthly Review Press

Fuller, Bruce (1991) Growing-up Modern, The Western State Builds Third World *Schools.* New York: Rutledge

Jansen, Jonathan (2011) *We Need to Talk.* South Africa: Bookstorm & Macmillan

Jansen, Jonathan (2013) *We Need to Act.* South Africa: Bookstorm & Macmillan

Lemma, Brook (2006) Plasma television teachers – when a different reality takes over African education. In Dahlström, Lars &Mannberg, Jan (Eds) *Critical Educational Visions and Practices in Neo-liberal Times.* Umeå University: Global South Network Publisher

Nyambe, John (2008) Education Reform under Strangulation. In Compton, Mary & Weiner, Lois (Eds) *The Global Assault on Teaching, Teachers, and their Unions – Stories for Resistance.* New York: Palgrave Macmillan.)

Salvoj Zizek (2013) In short, Madiba was not Mugabe. *Mail &Guardian*, December 13 to 19,page 33

Tabulawa, Richard (2003) International Aid Agencies, Learner-centred Pedagogy and Political Democratisation: a critique. *Comparative Education*, Volume 39, No 1. 7-26.

Tamatea, Laurence (2005) The Dakar Framework: constructing and deconstructing the global neo-liberal matrix. *Globalization, Societies and Education*, Volume 3, Number 3. 311-344

5 Neoliberal capitalism and dismantling public education in India

Ravi Kumar

THE BEHEMOTH called neoliberal capital is on its unabashed march demolishing anything that is human, transforming everything into a tradable commodity. Neoliberal capital is slimy, cunning and desperate to make profit with the least possible investment. Hence, it invests in sectors such as electricity, education and health, gets subsidised land and other facilities from state. It does not invest anywhere, except as a mistake, which would culminate in a financial loss. It is ready to bring everything within the ambit of the market, the only condition being its promise of generating profit. India, today, is pursuing this in the most unabashed manner along with the *rhetoric* of social justice, poverty elimination and economic betterment – the reality is different. As the number of private institutions within education increase, the idea of social justice such as affirmative action for the oppressed castes and tribes gets negated.

In India, there is an increasing trend towards privatising all state-managed services. This is not a new phenomenon but began much earlier when the state declared that it could not educate everyone or provide healthcare to every citizen. State expenditure on education remains around 3% of Gross Domestic Product (GDP) and that on health hardly ever went beyond 2% of GDP (see Table 1). There has been an overall trend to make education a commodity suitable for private capital to trade like any other item available in market for consumption.

Table 1: Expenditure on Health and Education as % of GDP
Source: Economic Survey of different years

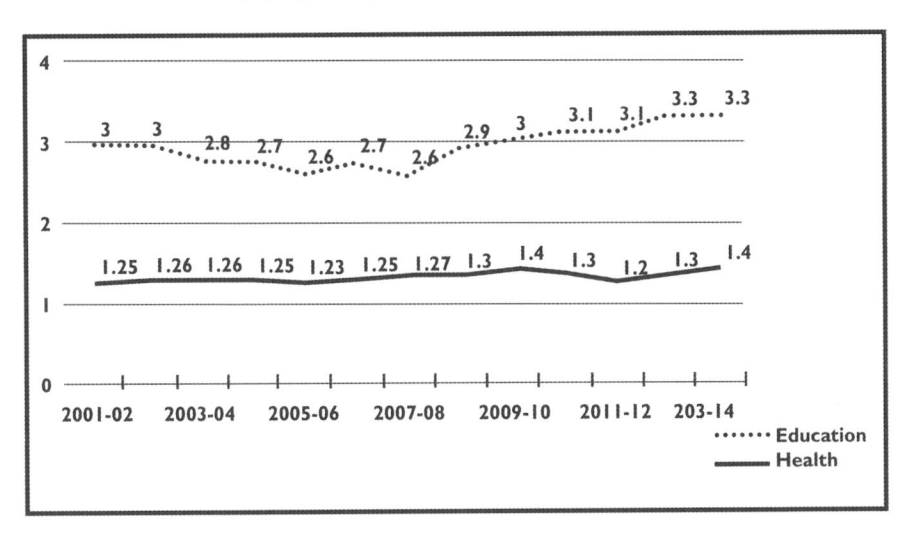

Year	Education	Health
2001-02	3	1.25
2003-04	3	1.26
2005-06	2.8	1.26
2007-08	2.7	1.25
2009-10	2.6	1.23
2011-12	2.7	1.25
203-14	2.6	1.27
	2.9	1.3
	3	1.4
	3.1	1.3
	3.1	1.2
	3.3	1.3
	3.3	1.4

The Indian state, along with private capital, international agencies such as World Bank and United Nation in connivance with pro-market intellectuals began a concerted process of delegitimising the state-managed schools on grounds of insufficient infrastructure, teacher absenteeism, teacher unionism etc. None of these players ever said that children across class, caste, religion and gender cannot be well educated unless there is a predominantly state-managed education system in the country. They rather began telling everybody that the option was to move towards privatisation, contractualisation of teaching labour force (see Table no.2) and sub-contractualisation of facilities such as mid-day meals and computer education. This has a different picture across the country but there are federal states which figure worse than the all India figure, specifically at the primary education level. Hence, studies were conducted to show that contractual teachers were better than regular teachers as they were 'more likely to be present in school and more engaged in teaching task", forgetting that those doing studies themselves wouldn't survive on the meagre salary that these teachers get. They earn anywhere between Rs.500/- (approximately $8.5) to Rs.10,000/- (approx. $167) per month or maybe a little more. Because of the federal character of India, these wages differ from state to state. There is no national law ensuring uniformity in wages. The pimps of private capital celebrate whenever the number of contractual workers increase in the education sector (or for that matter any other sector).

Table 2: Percentage of Para/contract teachers to the total teachers in different categories (2009)
Source: Collated from 8th All India Education Survey of National Council of Educational Research and Training

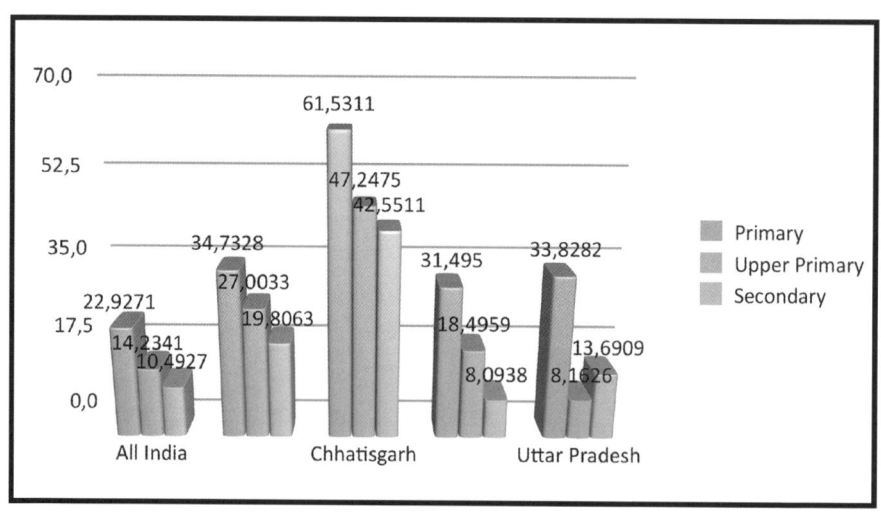

Category	All India	Chhatisgarh	Uttar Pradesh
Primary	22,9271	61,5311	33,8282
Upper Primary	14,2341	47,2475	18,4959
Secondary	10,4927	42,5511	13,6909
(additional)	34,7328	27,0033	31,495
(additional)	17,5	19,8063	8,0938
			8,1626

Because education across the world is experiencing similar developments it can be very well said that neoliberalism is not a localized phenomenon – the difference lies in its magnitude and form. In essence it is the rule of private capital which does the same thing everywhere – destroys the idea of commons and anything which seems antithetical to the market, and embarks on a ruthless campaign to bring every aspect of our life into the sphere of the market. If there is the slightest hint of solidarity among workers – teachers of educational factories or the motorbike and car factories – all of them are met with the same aggression and violence jointly sponsored by the state.

Another factor has been the weakness of the teacher unions themselves in the face of these assaults. In particular, this relates to the failure of these unions, in spite of their left leadership, to mobilise and struggle against the contractualisation process when it began. Some even initially praised reports that recommended how 'good' education could be with reduced state expenditure. This failure to mobilise has created an unspoken hierarchy between 'permanent' and contractualised teachers, with left-led unions only recently moving to unionise contractual teachers.

The unionisation of contractual teachers that has happened has been largely outside left politics. They are predominantly members of 'independent' non-political unions who would appeal to different parties in power to hike their wages and improve their working conditions, but without a broader critique of what is happening in education. This might be a reflection of a larger problem of left unionisation, which has struggled with the question of how to unionise the informalised workforce in general.

Overall, there is a heightened surveillance within educational institutions. Everybody within the campuses, is under constant scrutiny. Universities like University of Delhi have shown in the recent past that institutional frameworks can be altered radically in favour of the market if a Vice-Chancellor so desires. Academics, working as agents within the administration, such as Deans etc., the legal institutions as well as the executive come together to redefine an institution in the most autocratic manner. It becomes suffocating when you are not allowed to hold academic debates within institutions or not permitted to carry a camera at particular public spaces. This is what has happened in many institutions across the country. The idea of representative democracy has either become a farce within these institutions or is being done away with entirely.

Today, the situation is much grimmer. There won't be any respite from the anti-worker neoliberal aggression. It will, in all probability, increase as the Indian state takes up corporate ethics as its way of working. This is done in the name of reducing bureaucracy and more focused emphasis on development. However, this is obviously the capitalist development of ensuring that corporate capital does not have to face any obstacles to getting what it wants – ranging from control over natural resources to free subsidies (out of tax payers money) from the state to manage an electricity company and sell back electricity at an exorbitant price to the people.

This rule of corporate capital is supplemented by neo-conservative tendencies that would teach students that stem cell research happened thousands years back in India as per Hindu mythology[2] and emphasise how India is a Hindu nation.[3] There is no contradiction between the neoliberal capital's rule and neo-conservative tendencies because while the former keeps talking about new and innovative ideas the latter tends to create a mass base through Hindu rhetoric to be used whenever corporate capital requires it. This was visible when during the 2014 elections the cadres of the right-wing

Rashtriya Swamsevak Sangh (RSS) went from house to house asking for votes for Narendra Modi while corporate houses funded the blitzkrieg campaign of the Bhartiya Janata Party (BJP). [4]

This presents a difficult situation where the cadre politics, which is deeply ideological, becomes the backbone of the consensus creation process for neoliberal capital. The 2014 General Elections have shown the power of right-wing cadre politics that came through the Rashtriya Swamsevak Sangh (RSS) members. The resistance against the pauperization of the teaching work force and the dismantling of public education, therefore, becomes difficult. This difficulty is furthered because of the historically short-sighted politics of the left in the country. For them education never became a site of ideological battle against capital and hence, they neither prepared their teacher cadre to participate in the battle to create a pedagogy and curriculum for revolution. Not only this, there has been the historical fallacy of discounting teachers as 'workers', which led to the emergence of labour 'aristocracy' among teachers. Teachers do not fight with same vigour for the contractual gardeners, sweepers, etc., in the educational system. At a more ideological level there has not been much meaningful working class intervention in the traditional-conservative constructs within education such as that of the teachers themselves. In contemporary times the weak or non-existent alliance between the permanent and contractual teachers is a result of this kind of politics that has been followed by the left, 'progressive' forces. There is an increasing need to take the struggle within the educational institutions to the outside world where they fight in alliance with other workers and become part of the larger struggles of working class. It is important that alternatives are created as weapons in this battle where the insatiable appetite of capital seeks to devour everything and transform everything into commodities. The process of creating alternatives as an exercise in conscientisation and politicization, as a rupture that fosters creative minds, is an important political task in this situation.

Footnotes

1   Look at Kingdon, Geeta Gandhi & Sipahimalani-rao, Vandana (2010) Para-Teachers in India: Status and Impact, *Economic and Political Weekly*, Vol XLV, No.12, p.66

2   http://indianexpress.com/article/india/gujarat/science-lesson-from-gujarat-stem-cells-in-mahabharata-cars-in-veda/

3   http://indianexpress.com/article/india/india-others/india-is-a-hindu-nation-and-hindutva-is-its-identity-says-rss-chief-mohan-bhagwat/

4   http://www.hindustantimes.com/StoryPage/Print/1207499.aspx?s=p

Interlude Pearson's New Clothes

To mark the annual shareholders meeting of Pearson - the biggest corporate beast in the GERM jungle - TS wrote a fairy story:

Once upon a time, there were some clever merchants who travelled the world persuading rulers, who were usually stupid but ruthless, to make clothes by a wonderful new method. All they had to do was buy the patent, which would cost a squillion gold pieces, but my goodness it would be worth it.

'These wonderful clothes will keep all your people warm', they said. 'Forget the tailors who are making the clothes at the moment. They're rubbish. If they won't make our sort of clothes, sack 'em and get some people in who will. They don't need training. They just need to do it exactly like we tell them to. Because our clothes are world-class and they'll solve all your problems and make everyone happy and end poverty and generally bring about heaven on earth.'

But the rulers, who secretly didn't much like the look of the new clothes said, 'Do we have to wear them?'

And the merchants said, 'Don't be silly, of course you don't – are we wearing them? Just get on and do as we say.'

So the rulers said, 'We will!' And they said to the people: 'Get rid of your old clothes and your rubbish old tailors if they won't do what we say, and put these on. They're great.'

And the old tailors were a bit sad, but they thought they'd better make the clothes like the merchants said, otherwise they might get their heads chopped off, which would be unpleasant. So they made the new clothes and they knew they were rubbish but they often said to the people: 'These will keep out the winter wind and keep you cool in summer and end poverty and generally be world-class.' And the people were a bit fed up because the clothes were rubbish and they didn't fit and they were made of really cheap material and they were scratchy and they fell apart and they certainly didn't bring about heaven on earth.

Then one day, one of the tailors said to another tailor: 'You know what? – these clothes are rubbish.'

And the other tailor said, 'You're right'. And some of the leading tailors were really shocked because they were frightened of the merchants and they kind of believed that the new clothes were world-class and would end poverty and bring about heaven on earth.

But the tailors talked to other tailors and then to tailors in other lands and they all agreed. 'These clothes are rubbish and we're not going to make them anymore!'

And the people agreed too and said, 'These clothes are rubbish and we're not going to wear them anymore.'

And the rulers scratched their heads and said to the merchants, 'What do we do now?'

And the merchants said, 'Buggered if we know.'

So the tailors decided to get together with the people and design new clothes which really would make life better. They were all different: some countries had stripy clothes and some had spotty ones and people who lived near the North Pole wore warm clothes and people who lived in Italy wore very very fashionable ones, and some clothes were good for dancing and some for running and some just for sitting down and thinking about the world.

So the clever merchants and the stupid but ruthless rulers scratched their heads and slithered back to middle earth and everyone was jolly glad they'd gone. And because the people were wearing such good clothes which helped them to dance and keep warm or to keep cool and think, they decided to block up the entrance to middle earth and see if another world wasn't possible.

6 Modernizing education reforms and the governmental policies against the teachers organization in Ecuador

Edgar Isch L.

IT's BEEN DECADES since the urgency for educational reforms was raised globally. Most of these reforms have taken place under neoliberal prescriptions, which in Latin American countries have been strongly driven by mechanisms of external debt. Thus, the bankers from the World Bank, the Inter-American Development Bank or the International Monetary Fund, assumed the role of educational administrators and counsellors of the reforms.

This is what happened in Ecuador from early 80's until 2007. But the national case had a special feature: the popular and indigenous organizations, including the teachers' union, were able to push a profound resistance that prevented the total implementation of neoliberal policies. Part of this struggle was the overthrow of three corrupt and anti-popular governments, all in a 10 year period.

In the field of the education, the popular resistance avoided the implementation of a series of neoliberal policies, but it was not enough to stop a coordinated attack on public education. For these reasons Ecuadorian education went into crisis, a crisis which successive governments have tried to blame on teachers.

The popular struggle led to the electoral victory of a government which was outwardly critical of neoliberalism and backed by social movements. This government, in the first moment took important actions and established constitutional principles that collected the social demands of the past decades. However, in a second moment, it identified itself with the search for a "modernization" which comprised strengthening capitalism with some social democratic measures.

President Correa himself has said: 'Let's be globalized to compare ourselves with the best ... to aspire being at the top: a system of higher education that can be among the best in the world." After that, it was directed to follow the hegemonic measures in developed countries: entrance exams for universities, standardized tests at every level, incorporation of the country to private programs such as the International Baccalaureate, PISA tests, universities ranking, almost total destruction of university autonomy, reduction of the importance of social courses to expand technical subjects, segregation of students between 'winners" and 'losers" among many others.

Ironically, this has been combined with increased funding for public education, which today receives more students than before, and with an extensive program of scholarships for young Ecuadorians to study at universities in other countries (at the present moment there are more than 8000 students on these programmes).

Following the neoliberal doctrine, the vision prevails that the educational system should be at the service of companies and their needs. This determines that State resources are serving private interests. Even a new university created as a 'City of Knowledge" is directed to conduct the research that industry needs and to establish a center of private industrial development.

This, then, is a singular reform process. The modernization aim is posed as an imitation of the supposedly "successful" countries. The government leaves aside the democratic principle that education, particularly university, should respond in first place to the social problems of the country and the cultural particularities.

This text tries to explain in a summarized way the uniqueness of the Ecuadorian case and highlights the urgent need for solidarity with the teachers' union (UNE), one of the popular organizations operating under government pressure.

The national context

Alexander Von Humboldt said that Ecuador was occupied by 'poor people surrounded by a rich land". The conditions of social inequality make this sentence, expressed in the nineteenth century, still true today. There is a big contrast between the enormous natural wealth and tradition of the working people, and an unfair distribution of wealth which generates massive poverty.

The policy currently applied in Ecuador has become a topic of interest in different parts of the world because the government expresses its opposition to neoliberalism; but, at the same time, the government is identified with a new administrative form of capitalism without fundamentally changing the unfair distribution of wealth and extent of class, gender, ethnic and regional inequalities (Isch, 2011).

In education, similarly to other social aspects, it is necessary to consider three periods: the neoliberal, with serious effects on public education; the post-neoliberal in the first governmental period of Rafael Correa, including changes in favour of public education and the most disadvantaged people; and a third period, affirming a policy of modernisation of capitalism and a reinforcement of social inequalities, differently from the neoliberal phase.

This differentiates Ecuador from most countries in the world in which neoliberalism continues to be radically applied. The government has made some breaks with neoliberal policies but, on the other hand, reinforces a number of continuities with the same conflicts that these generate (of course with different levels and conditions).

A peculiarity is that the government is responding to what are fundamentally social and labour conflicts through the courts. For this, the government uses laws of the military dictatorship of the 70s, which have not been used previously even by neoliberal governments. This explains the existence of around 200 leaders of social organizations, including teachers, who have been accused by the government on charges of sabotage and terrorism (Cano, 2010). Their real crime has been fulfilling their role in defending collective rights. Given that we are talking about a country where there is no organisation that can be designated as a terrorist organisation and no organisations calling for armed struggle, this shows that what we are experiencing is a process of criminalisation of social struggle.

On other hand, thanks to the increase of the international prices of oil and other raw materials exported by Ecuador, the government has had access to an amount of monetary resources like no other before. Also, it should be added that (in the first phase of the government) the policy against external debt ended in a major renegotiation and recovery of resources for the state, as well as the expansion of the population paying taxes, also generating more resources for the national treasury.

This has enabled a series of populist policies expressed through money that is given to the poor, along with increases in spending in the social area. However, in recent years social spending, especially on health and education, has failed to deliver the increases ordered by the Constitution of the Republic and there exists a social debt owed by the government.

According to an official document (Atlas of socioeconomic inequalities of Ecuador) 'Social conditions have improved slowly during the 1990s, and that change has accelerated between 2001 and 2010". The same can be said about the eradication of poverty or increasing education coverage especially in high school.

Consequently, we see a complex situation that can be described as a reformist and developmentalist government. The developmentalist aspect is based on an economy of production of raw materials for the exportation and extractive sector, which has tied the country into the dictates of the international market. The government has stated that "we will leave the extractive sector with major extractive production" and advertises new universities and measures that aim to copy the educational accomplishments of the so-called "developed" countries.

The neoliberal modernizing reforms and their transformation in the current developmentalist reforms

The neoliberal stage

Ecuador was characterized by a high quality public school system until the end of the 1960s, managing to have one of the highest percentages of coverage in Latin America.

Under the neoliberal phase, starting in 1982, the targets outlined in the educational plans and programs were not achieved. For example, in tests on student knowledge in the basic areas conducted under the name of "Aprendo" in 1996 and 2000, there was a decline in student's scores despite the development of programs financed by external debt. Of course, the quality to which reference is made in these policies and projects is tied to the value of the "product, not by virtue of its objective characteristics, but the subjective perception of the customer" (Estévez Pérez, 2010, p. 22).

This was used to take the educational process even further down the road of ideologically-driven neoliberal reform, to allow privatization and school segregation, but not to meet the needs of the broadest sectors of the population. The neoliberal language inserted in the educational process involved major changes in educational conceptions of teachers and parents, who were increasingly approached from a business perspective, and moved discourse away from a pedagogical understanding of the teaching-learning process (Isch L., 2001).

The educational reforms, based on the recipes of the World Bank and Inter-American Bank, had the characteristics of processes imposed from outside the country and outside the realities of educational institutions, with the aim of transforming without any social consultation. They were technocratic reforms, removed from reality, which saw education as an isolated area, separate from other state responsibilities. The educational system was located within the general proposals of an administrative decentralisation but without any element of democratisation, justifying the separation between education for the poorest and the wealthiest. Thus, it can be said that the intention was to encourage a fundamentally different education for different social classes.

In Ecuador, the educational policies of the 1990s were imposed mainly by projects financed with loans from the foreign debt. The Committee for the Integral Audit of Public Credit (Isch L., 2008) included in their work educational credits that were more influential in education policies than the Ministry of Education itself which popularly became known as the 'poor ministry', versus the 'rich ministry" represented by the projects of international debt.

An analysis of this period shows that the imposition of neoliberal policies has affected the human right to education in a variety of ways, causing changes regardless of national interests and the laws, creating an economic support from the state budget to the private sector through payment mechanisms, and finally without generating a better quality education, which in fact is confirmed in the reports of the managers of these projects themselves (Isch L., 2008).

The conclusions of this study showed the negative effects of these credits and related projects, while it was noted that: 'quitting the burden of debt must also mean quitting the application of neoliberalism in education; after putting aside the educational and administrative reforms imposed from this standpoint and from multilateral banks, then you find an education that meets our reality (...) '(Isch , 2008, p. 26). Unfortunately, the current government ministry officials have not challenged these projects, which may be understandable if one considers that the most important official in the area of education in the government of Rafael Correa has been the former minister Raúl Vallejo (Minister between January 2007 and April 2010), who had served as Minister of Education (1991 and 1992) in another government that encouraged this type of projects, led by Rodrigo Borja, just as it was in the government of Alfredo Palacio (2005-2006).

Some data indicators of this crisis, presented by UNICEF (2006), show high levels of dropouts, extremely bad conditions in two out of ten schools, underpaid teachers and the permanent reduction of the educational budget from 5.4 % of GNP 1981, to 1.8% of GNP in 2000. Of the 1,657,963 primary school students (for the year 1999-2000), only 356,837 received textbooks, mostly from local governments and non from the central State.

The early years of the present government

The social struggle for education allowed the development of three National Consultations, entitled 'Education XXI Century "; in which important agreements were achieved with the participation of various sectors of Ecuadorian society. The First Consultation (1992) established the 'Basis of the National Agreement', which was supplemented in the Second Consultation, held in 1996. The agreements reached, however, were not considered by various governments, leading to the realization of a third consultation that sought to be less ambitious and more pragmatic in setting specific goals.

The debate focused serious attention on education and resulted in the first Ten Year Plan 2006-2015. The eight policies of this plan were approved by referendum on November 26th, 2006, with the support of all sectors of education and most social organizations, although some of the parties identified with the neoliberal politics abstained from voting. The Ten-Year Plan was approved by more than 66% of voters and opposed by less than 8%.

When Rafael Correa started his government with this popular mandate, the Ten Year Plan became largely the core of its educational proposal. However, just a few references are published about it on the website of the Ministry of Education.

One of the commitments of the new government was the development of a National Constituent Assembly that was held in the city in Montecristi, between November 30, 2007 and July 25, 2008. The social mobilization and debate around this Assembly were very high and reflected the views of the existing social classes in the country. The Assembly, most members of which belonged to the democratic and leftist parties, achieved a Constitution that is recognized as "warranty of rights" and reflects a "new constitutionalism".

The Constitution was approved by a Constitutional referendum on September 28, 2008, with the support of 63.93 % of the citizens. One of the most important aspects is a new system of development called Sumak Kawsay (translated as 'Good Live'), that speaks about fair coexistence between humans and between society and nature, promoting collective solidarity (Ecuador, 2008).

Sumak Kawsay, like the definition of Ecuador as multinational State, continues to be a proposal that must be filled with content, recognizing the Andean ancestral knowledge but also determining more precisely the scope and terms of the social life.

On education, the Constitution proposes, among other things:
- Education is a right of people throughout life and inescapable and inexcusable duty of the State. (Art. 26).
- Education will focus on human beings and must ensure their holistic development, respect for human rights, a sustainable environment and democracy; it will be mandatory, intercultural, inclusive and diverse; it will promote gender equality, justice, solidarity and peace; (...) Education is essential for knowledge, the exercise of rights, building a sovereign country and is a strategic area for national development (Art. 27).
- Universal access, retention, mobility and exit without discrimination will be ensured as well as the obligatory studies in the initial, basic and high school level or equivalent (Art. 28).
- Public education will be universal and secular (separation between religion and state) at all levels (Art. 28).
- The state will guarantee freedom of education and the right of indigenous people to learn in their own language and cultural environment (Art. 29).
- The State shall guarantee to teachers at all levels and modalities, stability, training, educational and academic improvement, fair pay, according to the professionalism,

performance and academic merit. The law shall regulate the educational and career ladder, establish a national system of performance evaluation and wage policy at all levels (Art. 349).

Together, the Teachers National Union (UNE), the Ecuadorian High School Students Federation (FESE), the Ministerial Technical – Teachers Federation, the Principals National Association, the Association of Faculties of Philosophy and Education Sciences, popular educators and others carried out from 23 to 27 April 2007, the Second National Congress on Public Education. At that event the mandate 'Educating for freedom, educating for New Homeland"(UNE-MEC , 2007), which was largely reflected in constitutional principles, was adopted.

Taking up the highlights of the early years, the significant increase in social investment as a percentage of GDP must be appreciated, which has as a first factor the huge growth in government revenue due to the price of oil, the main export product of Ecuador and also a government decision to reduce the burden of external debt in the budget. Social investment went from 4.8 % of GDP in 2006 to 4.9% in 2014.

Additionally, in 2006 social investment represented 0.35 times the external debt service, while in 2009 became 2.63 times the debt service.

With the new educational budget, the mandatory payment made by the parents of $25 for every child who was enrolled in public schools was eliminated. This payment officially was called 'voluntary" contribution but acted as a barrier for thousands of children and teenagers who were left out the education system. In addition to this, the benefits of public schools grew, especially in the poorest areas, like school breakfasts and lunches (although last year the lunch was removed to provide an 'enhanced breakfast'). Free uniforms were given to students in rural schools and about 3 million textbooks for students in basic general education.

The current situation

These developments contrast with the negative factors that remain. The first arises because there is teacher labour flexibility. Of the 147,129 teachers from the national education system until 2013, only 99,611 have labour stability, while 47,518 work under the category of 'temporary employment contract"with a monthly salary between $430 and $530. The Ministry has attempted hiring professionals in other countries without having the desired response, despite the fabulous salaries offered ranging from $2,226 up to $5,009.

According to the Ministry of Education, the country has 102,247 teachers but will need 160,000 teachers by 2017.

All teachers can apply for reclassification or promotion, which should have been completed in 2011 and still has not taken place. Some 43,640 teachers are in category G, whose salary is $817 a month. The reclassification is considered as an exceptional action that puts teachers in the category that corresponds to them according to their merits and rights.

Meanwhile, the National State Budget currently has $3,700 million, which corresponds 4.9% of GDP, earmarked for education. This violates the constitutional mandate that orders that a minimum of 6% of GDP is allocated to education. That means a shortfall of $1,900 million owed to education.

Another negative aspect is the lack of appropriate facilities. Whilst the government is constructing "schools of the millennium"(technology endowed schools), Ecuador has nearly 30,000 educational institutions, of which just 7,758 own computer labs; 1,280 science labs and 205 language labs (AMIE, 2009-2010).

Evaluation policies have returned to the standardised procedures that ignore the diversity of cultural and social conditions. This is particularly serious when the fact that 'the greatest inequalities are among students from different socio-economic levels" and that "ethnic minority students also remained disadvantaged" are considered (Grupo FARO, 2010). The National Assessment and Accountability (SER) has sought to assess exclusively teachers and students, without taking any account of contextual factors, always highlighting a supposed superiority of private education. Its use, however, has meant the introduction of other instruments of segregation, including in late 2010 some high schools only enrolling those with high scores, putting out students with lower scores. Many of these children work four hours or more every day to support families living in poverty.

In terms of quality, the government highlights some facts (El ciudadano, 2011) that add challenges to those made by the lack of a comprehensive educational proposal at the end of seven years of government. Among the factors that the authorities tend to mention are:

- A proposal for a new high school which is opposed by different institutions for its "inconsistency, improvisation, arbitrariness, incoherence" ... "The proposal disrupts 'Education for Democracy" and suppresses the Environmental Education and National Reality" (Andean University 'Simón Bolívar", 2011). 'In the proposal of the General Unified School, education is approached as a training to do things and not to think or discern"said the rector Enrique Ayala (La Hora, 2011).
- The so-called Strengthening Curriculum of Basic General Education, which is essentially an adaptation of the content since 1996 and is guided by the achievement of 'skills with performance criteria". There is no real curriculum change in the process.
- Continuity of free education, an achievement that is weakening. There are complaints of charges to parents.
- ●Schools of the millennium", no more than 40 in all the country, equipped with the latest technology, while there are schools that are literally falling on their students. In 2009 school infrastructure in the country was rated with 3.3 points out of 10 (Expreso, 2009).
- The project to introduce the 'International Baccalaureate (IB)", for a few public high schools. This has broken into two high schools so far, always attacking national education (Isch L., 2008b).

As you can conclude, these changes, carried out in individual projects, marking the exception and not the general rule, are the way new forms of educational discrimination are created, all in the name of a "meritocracy"which works in favour of those who have better living conditions.

A comprehensive study confirms this remark: "In fact, the construction of a comprehensive and integrated public education policy for youth and adults is in the making, as the formulation of public policy to address the educational backwardness sustained where children, adolescence, youth and adult population are"(Amaluisa, 2011, p. 18).

The union response

There is a single union of teachers with a national structure, which is recognized as one of the largest trade associations in the country. This is the Teachers National Union (UNE), which includes about 90,000 teachers working in different educational levels. The union is member of Education International.

Membership of the UNE was traditionally mandatory but Rafael Correa's government has taken some measures against the unions, among which was the elimination of mandatory affiliation. Therefore, the Ecuadorian teachers had to develop a process of seeking voluntary membership which mobilized most of the teachers in the country to defend their organization.

Another measure taken against UNE was to suspend the direct economic contributions that their affiliates gave to maintain the organization. In a difficult process, it has been necessary to establish payment systems through private banks, confirming the grassroots support of the union and its leadership. Additionally, the government has banned the development of trade union activities in state educational establishments, calling them political acts that destabilize the democratic regime.

With similar intentions, the government eliminated the permit time for union activity. This means that today our leaders must work every day for eight hours in their educational establishments and, after that period, travel to the union headquarters to carry out their trade union activities.

Additionally, there is a process of criminalization of social protest. In the educational system there are three concrete measures: prohibition of strikes or teachers' participation in protest activities during working time; the ban on school principals from making public statements (the dismissal of UNE's president of the province of Guayas was justified on these grounds); prosecution of leaders who develop critical activities or opposition to government policies.

One of the most serious cases is against Mery Zamora, who as national president of the UNE attended a school to carry out her role coincidentally on September 30, 2010, while a national police strike was taking place. Mery Zamora has been charged with "sabotage and terrorism" and sentenced to eight years in prison, which would begin at the end of her legal defence.

A few months ago a delegation from the International Education of Latin America (IE-AL) was in Ecuador to analyse the case and concluded that there is a process of political persecution that demands international solidarity. This issue began in the middle of a teacher union strike that achieved important victories (Isch L., 2010) when President Correa called for the creation of another teacher organisation, and the official newspaper *The Telegraph* (27 January 2009) announced 40,000 members of the 'new union'. This was never real and produced a political defeat of the regime.

It is important to say that government anti-union measures were taken after the government changed its relation with most of the popular organizations and political left. This happened despite the fact that the President has maintained leftist rhetoric in some forums. However in other forums, Correa has declared that he is neither anti-capitalist nor anti-imperialist (as he said on the visit to Ecuador of Hilary Clinton); that in terms of wealth accumulation the government will do the same as before but better, and that he does not want to affect wealthy people.

Even policies that go directly against government commitments made in campaigns and against the constitution often come under a supposedly leftist discourse.

Lessons from the Ecuadorian experience

The experience of the Teachers National Union highlights the strength achieved through democratic mechanisms of functioning and the importance of union autonomy from both political power and economic power. Recent UNE national elections to nominate the National Executive Committee (December 2013), involving more than 70% of teachers in public education, were a demonstration of the active life of the union and the support of their social base throughout the country.

Government policy against popular organizations and, specifically against the Teachers National Union, has weakened the capacity of mobilization without doubt, but it was not enough to destroy independent trade unions, as has been their purpose in recent years. This is also reflected in the fact that to this day the government has failed to build an organisation of teachers to respond to presidential terms.

The experience, in general, demonstrates the need for a teachers union to defend human and labour rights, but also to develop a capacity for advocacy on the educational policies of governments and to stop the imposition of neoliberal reforms. The UNE is committed to an "education for liberation" involving also fights for social and national emancipation. Therefore UNE is confronting the developmentalist and extractivist policies that reinforce dependence of the country on global capital and maintain the mechanisms of accumulation of social wealth in few hands.

It is clear that in the struggle for human rights, there is a long way to go. But, the experience of the Ecuadorian people's organizations raises their fighting ability, strength and offensive for emancipation. International solidarity is an important factor to strengthen the capacity of grassroots organizations and urgently to protect the life and liberty of honest union leaders who are accused of crimes they did not commit.

References

AMALUISA FIALLOS, C. Rezago educativo: barrera a vencer para el buen vivir. Quito: Contrato Social por la Educación, 2011. (Cuadernos del Contrato Social por la Educación, n. 6).

AMIE, 2009-2010. Archivo maestro de instituciones educativas 2009-2010.

APRENDO. Resultados nacionales de la aplicación de las pruebas aprendo 1996 (redes CEM del EB/PRODEC). Quito: Ministerio de Educación y Cultura, 1998.

APRENDO. Resultados nacionales de la aplicación de las pruebas aprendo 2000 (redes CEM del EB/PRODEC). Quito, Ministerio de Educación y Cultura, 2000.

BANCO MUNDIAL. Evaluación final de EB/PRODEC. 2000.

CANO, J. Terrorismo made in Ecuador. Revista Vanguardia, Quito, n. 267, nov. 2010.

CONTRATO SOCIAL POR LA EDUCACIÓN. Indicadores educativos del Ecuador. 2011. Disponible en: http://www.contratosocialecuador.org.ec>

CORREA, R. Video. 2010. Disponible en: http://www.youtube.com/watch?v=x-ProShvE5s

ECUADOR. ASAMBLEA NACIONAL. Ley Orgánica de Educación Intercultural. 2011. Disponible en: www.asambleanacional.gov.ec.

ECUADOR. Constitución de la República del Ecuador; publicada en el registro oficial de 20 oct. Quito, 2008.

EL CIUDADANO. 2010, año de la revolución educativa. El ciudadano.gob.ec, (periódico digital del gobierno de la revolución ciudadana), 14 ene. 2011.

ESTÉVEZ PÉREZ, S. Destrucción de la enseñanza científica. Quito: Causa Proletaria; MIR, 2010.

GENTILI, P. Neoliberalismo e educação: manual do usuário. In: SILVA, T.T.; Gentili, P. (Org.). Escola S.A.: quem ganha e quem perde no mercado educacional do neoliberalismo. Brasília, DF: CNTE, 1996.

GRUPO FARO. Informe de progreso educativo Ecuador: ¿Cambio educativo o educación por el cambio? Quito: Grupo FARO; PREAL; Fundación Ecuador, 2010. Disponible en: http://www.educacion.gov.ec/

INSTITUTO NACIONAL DE ESTADÍ STICAS Y CENSOS (INEC). Ecuador en cifras 2009. Disponible en: http://www.inec.gov.ec/web/guest/inicio.

ISCH LÓPEZ, E. Educación democrática para enfrentar a la educación neoliberal. Quito: Pedagógicas; Ibarra, 2001.

ISCH LÓPEZ, E. BM y BID: deuda para imponer la política neoliberal en educación; comisión para la auditoría integral del crédito público. Quito: Ministerio de Finanzas, 2008a.

ISCH LÓPEZ, E. Bachillerato internacional: ¿alternative o modelo extranjerizante? 2008b. Disponible en: http://www.voltairenet.org/article156513.html

ISCH LÓPEZ, E. Apuntes sobre la lucha del magisterio ecuatoriano contra la evaluación estandarizada. Intercambio, México, DF, v. 3, n. 1, jul. 2010.

ISCH LÓPEZ, E. ¿Qué clase de gobierno es éste? Elementos para caracterizar al segundo gobierno de Rafael Correa. Revista Rupturas, Quito, 2011.

LA HORA. El bachillerato unificado bajo lluvia de críticas. Diario La Hora, Quito, 9 mar. 2011.

LUNA TAMAYO, M. La educación en los últimos años en el Ecuador: situación y propuestas., Quito: Contrato social por la educación, 2006. (Cuadernos del Contrato Social por la Educación, n. 4)

ECUADOR. Ministerio de Educación. Actualización y fortalecimiento curricular de Educación Básica. Quito, 2009a. Disponible en: http://www.educacion.gov.ec/pages/interna_noticias.php?txtCodiNoti=1776. Aceso en: 25 ago. 2009.

ECUADOR. Ministerio de Educación. Rendición de Cuentas – año 2008: otro año de revolución educativa. Quito, 2009b. Disponible en: http://www.educacion.gov.ec/_upload/rendicion.pdf. Aceso en: 25 feb 2009.

ECUADOR. Ministerio de Educación. Nuevo Bachillerato Ecuatoriano, versión preliminar. Quito, 2010b. Disponible en: www.bachillerato.ecuatoriano.gov.ec

ECUADOR. Ministerio de Educación y Cultura. Plan decenal de educación 2006-2015. Quito, 2006. Disponible en: http://www.educacion.gov.ec/_upload/PlanDecenaldeEducacion.pdf.

REYES, G. ¿Hacia dónde marcha la economía ecuatoriana en el año 2011?. Rupturas: Revista de investigación, análisis y opinión, Quito, n. 2, ene. 2011.

UNIÓN NACIONAL DE EDUCADORES. Propuesta de Educación para La emancipación. Quito: El Educador, 2008.

UNIÓN NACIONAL DE EDUCADORES. Posición de la UNE frente a la problemática educativa del país. Quito, 2009.

UNIÓN NACIONAL DE EDUCADORES. Resoluciones del segundo Congreso Nacional de la educación pública y mandato para la asamblea constituyente. Quito: UNE/ME, 2007.

UNICEF. ¿Qué país y que educación quieren los ecuatorianos?: Apuntes para un debate nacional. Quito, 2006.

UNIVERSIDAD ANDINA SIMÓN BOLÍVAR. Análisis de la propuesta de nuevo bachillerato presentada por el Ministerio de Educación. Área de Educación. Quito, 2011. Disponible en: www.uasb.edu.ec.

YACHAY (2013), ¿Que es Yachay? www.yachay.ec.

Footnotes

1   Regarding this fact it is questionable that a citizen is out of the poverty statistics by having revenues of $70 per month, while the basic family basket is over $587.30 per month.

2   Broadly speaking, the term "developmentalist" (in Spanish "desarrollismo") refers to theories and theoretical economic policies aimed at the modernization and industrialization of traditional economies, in the image and likeness of the 'developed' countries.

3   Similar to facilities time in the English and Welsh education systems – Ed.

4   see at Correa, 2010

5   interview on public newspaper published in January 2012

6   interview on public newspaper published in January 2012

7 Venezuela: education for the people

Francisco Dominguez

The hefty burden of neoliberal policies in Venezuela

THE PROGRESSIVE transformation of Venezuela has in 15 years involved drastic structural changes between state and society and between the state and the economy, but that has also involved the transformation of the Venezuelan people. No such transformation could be sustained for that long otherwise. In an amazing dialectical process in which the downtrodden, the driving social and political force of the Bolivarian process, not only push for radical transformations through mass activity, they themselves undergo an intellectual transformation by becoming increasingly conscious agents of the change they began to push for back on 27 February 1989, when they shook the foundations of oligarchic Venezuela by staging the now legendary mass uprising known as the *'Caracazo'*. Mass education has played a central role in this. This article seeks to chart the rich and multifaceted process of the education and self-education of the people of Venezuela aimed at creating a new citizen, and thus a new society.

Up to 1998 Venezuela was ruled by a regime pejoratively known as *puntofijismo* to signify the corrupt two party system (*Accion Democratica* and *COPEI*) of a parasitic oligarchy that lived off the siphoning off the country's oil revenues and which had run the nation since 1958. The old regime in Venezuela bequeathed an unsavoury legacy characterized by economic dependence, gross socio-economic inequalities, huge amounts of corruption, underdevelopment, poverty, squalor, illiteracy, and above all, the social and political exclusion of millions of ordinary Venezuelans. In fact, the *adecocopeyanos* (supporters of AD and COPEI) left the country in ruins, and burdened with a huge debt.[1] The ancient regime was so discredited that by 1989 it began to disintegrate of its own accord, so much so that it was beyond repair. Hugo Chavez, who was democratically elected in December 1998, was rightly convinced that the old regime, the thoroughly corroded IV Republic, had to be fully replaced lock, stock and barrel, by the V Republic, whose historic task was to lay the foundations for the rebuilding of the nation on the bases of a participatory democracy tasked with the full eradication of the ills and inequities associated with the neoliberal policies of oligarchic Venezuela. The state of the education of the people was consistent with such a description of the consequences of neoliberalism, thus by 1989 there were over 1.5 million people unable to read and write, extraordinarily high levels of primary and secondary school desertion, coupled with elitism and exclusion of large sections of society from higher education. Thus a Bolivarian government report showed that by the 1990s of every 100 children who enrolled in primary school, 91 reached third grade, 59 completed sixth grade, 38 ninth grade and barely 18 made it to second grade in secondary education. That is, of every 100 children that entered the schooling system in Venezuela, 32% were excluded before sixth grade, 53% before reaching ninth grade and 73% before they reached secondary school. To this must be added the even larger proportion of secondary school leavers who were unable to get into higher education because the number of places was insufficient.[2] In short, in line with the rest of the IV Republic regime, the education system was so designed as to exclude a very large proportion of Venezuela society from even getting the qualifications, education and skills to be able to participate, let alone compete in the labour market, consequently the level of informal workers in the economy by 1998 was well over 50% and poverty, another inexorable consequence of such a system, was 67% in 1996-97. [3]

It is, of course, not just education programmes that the Bolivarian government of Venezuela has relied upon to address the massive levels of inequality and social exclusion that existed in the country upon the coming to office of Hugo Chavez in 1998, but on a whole raft of social programmes and policies which have already produced extraordinary results. Official publications, from the Instituto Nacional de Estadisticas (National Institute of Statistics - INE), but also reports from highly prestigious bodies such as the Economic Commission for Latin America and the Caribbean (ECLAC) and the United Nations Development Programme (UNPD) confirm the tremendous progress being achieved. The former report indicates that Venezuela has the lowest percentage of social inequality in Latin America (0.38% - Venezuela's income per capita is US$10,000), whilst the latter shows that Venezuela has the lowest gender inequality index (0.56) in the region (0.6) [2011 UNDP REPORT]. Furthermore, the 2011 UNDP Report shows that in terms of the Human Development Index (HDI) Venezuela's is 0.735, above the regional average (it had been 0.646 in 1995). [4] Despite the enormous challenge that the plummeting of the prices of oil represents for Venezuela's economy, social progress has continued with the government increasing total social expenditure within the national budget from 61% in 2014 to 64% for 2015.[5]

We can gauge the overall impact of policies of social inclusion by also looking at the government created health programme called *Mision Barrio Adentro*, created in 2003, thanks to which 24 million Venezuelans, 80% of the population, are now served by 13,510 free public health centres (free care and free drugs are provided to 37,000 HIV-AIDS sufferers, and other expensive treatments, like cancer, are also subsidized by the government). In Venezuela poverty has been halved in 12 years of Bolivarian policies: from 43.9% of the households in 1998 to 26.9% in 2010; out of which 17.17% of the households were living in extreme poverty which by 2010 had declined to 6.9%. Poverty and extreme poverty have continued to decline further and in 2014 it affected 5.4% of households. Furthermore, 6,000 places have been set up to provide free food to low-income people and about 900,000 are benefiting daily and FAO recognises that by 2014 4,717,372 people have stopped suffering from hunger in Venezuela (Venezuela has also reached FAO's aim of 2,700 daily calories per person – it was 2,140 in 1998 and 2,790 in 2011). Thanks to the Bolivarian government policies on pensions the number of people who have been given a decent pension has gone from 387,000 in 1998 to 2,565,725 people in 2014. Last but not least, in the period 1999-2014 there have been 19 elections in Venezuela (more than in the previous 40 years before the coming to office of the Bolivarian government) where there is a well-structured opposition which is organised in over 60 political parties and has about 40% of Parliament seats, several governorships, mayoralties, local authorities, and municipalities. The opposition controls most of the TV stations, and the overwhelming majority of newspapers and radio stations. Thanks to the vigorous efforts by the Venezuelan government, the number of people registered to vote has increased from about 10 million in 1998 to about 20 million in 2015. [6] For the coming 2015 parliamentary elections the number of registered voters had gone up to nearly 20 million (http://www.cne.gov.ve/web/index.php). The Bolivarian government is not only not at all afraid of people expressing their will freely but vigorously and regularly encourages them to do so in an efficient and fraud-proof electoral system. In this latter regard Jimmy Carter, whose Carter Center has monitored elections in Venezuela, said: "As a matter of fact, of the 92 elections that we've monitored, I would say that the election process in Venezuela is the best in the world."[7]

Investing in education: Investing in the people – Investing in the future

In order to address the gross social deficit in education of the Venezuelan people, the government established various social education programmes aimed at achieving this objective. Thus, *Mission Robinson*, using the Cuban method *Yo Si Puedo* (Yes, I can) eradicated illiteracy (over 1.5 million people) in about one year and a half. This programme was followed by *Mission Robinson II*, aimed at adults who, due to their socio-economic reality had not been able to finish primary school. Then the government established *Mission Ribas* for working people who had been unable to finish their secondary education. And finally, there is *Mission Sucre*, for anybody especially workers who have completed secondary school and wish to undertake higher education. It must be stressed that every single one of these missions are totally free of charge and the law stipulates that it is employers, public or private, that must allow the necessary free time, without loss of pay, for people to undertake schooling and studies through any of these educational programmes.

The impact of the government's vigorous educational programmes has been enormous. Not only UNESCO certified the eradication of illiteracy in Venezuela in 2005, but there has been a substantial increase in all levels of schooling in the country such that between 1998 and 2014 the completion of initial education went from 43% to 77%; of primary education from 86% to 93%; of secondary education from 48% to 76%; and higher education went from 862,000 university students in 2000 to 2,692,312; that is, one in ten Venezuelans is undertaking university education and one in three is being educated. Furthermore, in the same period the Bolivarian government created 16 new universities, all free of charge, among them one for the Arts and another for Citizen's Safety and Security. And in Venezuela as whole there were over 29,000 fully functional educational establishments. [8] Since then the Bolivarian government has increased its commitment to social inclusion by putting greater resources into education, one of the key mechanisms to get people out of the vicious cycle of poverty and social exclusion.

The budget for education went from 3% of GDP in 1999 to 6% in 2011 and to 10% of GDP for the 2015 fiscal year with the country having about 12 million people undertaking education at some level. The policy of social inclusion involves not only offering extraordinary free-of-charge opportunities to millions of hitherto excluded individuals, it also involves offering educational opportunities to over 354,000 people with disabilities who have benefited from the José Gregorio Hernández Mission, especially created for that purpose. Thanks to the school meals programme – which provides two meals at school to 4 million children – infant malnutrition has been eradicated: 7.7% in 1999, 3.2% in 2010, and near 0% in 2014. Net enrolment rates increased by 28 per cent in nursery education for the same period. The total number of children and adolescents enrolled in school increased by 24 per cent between 1998 and 2010, standing at 7.7 million in the academic year 2009-2010, and by 2014 it was 10 million. UNESCO (2010) recognized Venezuela as the country with the fifth highest levels of higher education enrolment in the world and the second highest in Latin America and the Caribbean.

The 1999 Bolivarian Constitution of Venezuela is explicitly anti-neoliberal but it also grants the people the right to self-organise in order to make the general will prevail, creating the conditions for a participatory democracy. Furthermore, indigenous people enjoy special rights and, despite their small demographic weight, they have entitlement to their own parliamentary representation, and their culture is being actively promoted by the state. Similarly, under Chávez and since, Venezuela vigorously celebrates its African roots.

Inclusion and citizenship in Venezuela

The government has established *Infocentros* and made them available to the poor so that they also have access to modern telecommunications technologies. There are 820 Infocentros throughout Venezuela (810 of which have connectivity), 544 of which are connected to the Simón Bolívar and Francisco de Miranda satellites. Infocentros are important since in the digital age, a substantial part of humanity is excluded by being denied access to the speed and quantity of information processed digitally on a planetary scale. Additionally, access to digital sources represents a substantial improvement in the visibility of hitherto excluded citizens, but it also offers a much broader range of options for many economic, cultural, social, commercial and even political activities of individuals. The combination of modernisation and free of charge access to millions of Venezuelans, including access to sources of information about educational and training opportunities, enhances the participatory democracy that is being built in the country. The Regional distribution of *Infocentros* in Venezuela was in 2011 as shown in Figure 1

The total number of visits to use *Infocentros* in 2011 (Figure 2) alone was indeed very high, 12,344,714 (in 2001, when they began, it had been barely 1,335,647), thus showing a population enthusiastic and eager to catch up with innovation and use of the most modern technologies that the government makes freely available to them and which undoubtedly makes them feel included in society. By 2011 there were Infocentros in 85.6% of the municipalities of Venezuela as shown in Figure 2

Furthermore, *Infocentros* played a central role in the eradication of illiteracy in Venezuela. Between 2006 and 2011 the total number of people technologically alphabetised was 1,432,281 in a programme that also included people in prison. Its success was recognised internationally when, in December 2010, the Fundacion Infocentro received the UNESCO Rey Hamad Bin Isa Al Khalifa Prize in recognition of its contribution to the technological alphabetization of adults. The programme includes on-line literacy courses in Wayuunaki language for indigenous people. In the table we can see the distribution by state of those alphabetised technologically giving a picture of a technology that can have profound democratic possibilities and consequences since it has the potential to help develop educated, politically conscious, and well informed citizens.

State	Infocentro	Population	Inhabitants per Infocentro
Amazonas	14	157,293	11,235
Anzoategui	28	1,574,505	56,232
Apure	24	520,508	21,688
Aragua	27	1,574,505	58.315
Barinas	30	821,635	27,388
Bolívar	51	1,648,110	32,136
Carabobo	46	2,365,665	51,428
Cojedes	26	324,260	12,472
Delta Amacuro	9	166,907	18,545
Distrito Capital	68	2,109,166	31,017
Falcon	51	966,127	18,994
Guarico	22	802,540	36,479
Lara	39	1,909,846	48,790
Merida	34	907,938	26,704
Miranda	73	3,028,965	41,493
Monagas	44	926,478	21,056
Nueva Esparta	24	462,480	19,270
Portuguesa	46	942,555	20,940
Sucre	33	975,814	29,570
Tachira	42	1,263,628	30,086
Trujillo	25	765,946	30,638
Vargas	19	646,598	34,031
Yaracuy	34	342,845	10,084
Zulia	43	3,887,171	90,039
Infomoviles	28		
Total	852		

Figure 1 Regional distribution of *Infocentros* in Venezuela

Infocentros additionally contribute to the development of citizens' consciousness by providing on-line free-of-charge training and practical programmes to millions of ordinary Venezuelans, including text processing, multimedia, calculations and data in

Excel, surfing the internet, social networking, computer-generated presentations, PNAFT programme for the visually impaired: available in Infocentros in 22 out of the 24 Venezuelan states.

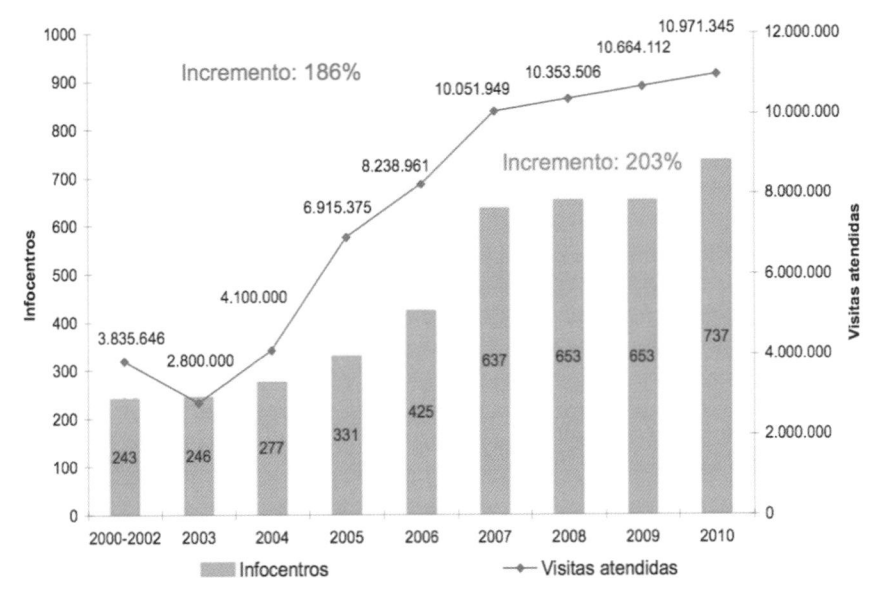

Figure 2 Attendance at Infocentros

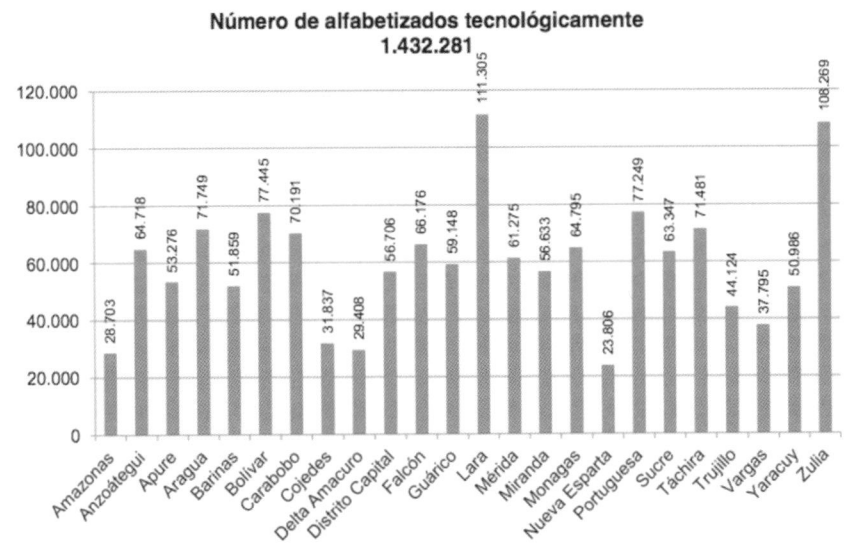

Figure 3 Eradicating illiteracy

Also there are on-line guides for treatment and classification of sources, creating digital photography collections, manipulation of images, publishing websites on the web, editing audio files, use and care of multimedia projectors and camcorders, publishing information on twitter, acquiring and circulating information through Google, computer-generated drawing, multimedia resources for video forums, how to look after your computer, etc. There are even on-line guides on how to generate specialist websites for tourism with a regional focus, communal commercial exchange, polls for *Infocentros*, community events, news and information of local communities' activities, digital newspapers, and how to improve writing, public speaking and spelling.

The government, wishing to ensure digital literacy from a tender age, has distributed, free of charge, nearly 4 million Canaima computers, entirely assembled in Venezuela for students to use in their education. The Venezuelan company that assembles them is Complejo Tecnologico Simón Rodríguez, named after the 19th century socialist thinker who was the personal tutor and mentor of Simón Bolívar and who played a decisive role in the radicalisation of his ideas.

Canaima computers have all the lessons, exercises, information and so forth for every level of education pupils go through, all of which is provided by the government totally free of charge. Pupils in the First Grade learn themes such as Indigenous Resistance, Bicentennial of Independence, Educators and Democracy, The protection of the Environment, Friendship, solidarity and love, Equality, fraternity and the environment, as well as Holidays, Christmas and Work and the family. Some of the slogans of the Canaima Project are: "Technology for a liberating education" and Simón Bolívar's 15 February 1808 dictum 'The first duty of a government is to educate the people". When pupils complete primary education they take their *Canaima* computer to an Infocentro were all the materials for their secondary school is uploaded, also totally free of charge.

All of the above has gone hand in hand with a staggering growth in telecommunications and telephony which reinforce directly and indirectly all the positive developments associated with Infocentros: access to digital information and the digitalization of education materials and learning. The table below compares the growth in telecommunications and telephony between 1998 and 2011, and also provides the net figures for 2013, thus showing that this development continues apace.[9]

Growth in telecommunications and telephony

	1998	2010	% variation	2013
Landline subscribers	2.517.220	7.054.603	280.25%	7,770,000
Mobile phones	2.009.757	29.152.847	1,450.53%	31,910,000
TV subscriptions	603.200	2.483.847	411.78%	4,674,614*
Internet users	322.244	9.956.842	3,089.85%	3,610,000

Broadening society's perception of itself – pedagogy of the oppressed on a national scale

One key principle of the Bolivarian government's approach to the transformation of Venezuela is the cultural betterment of the mass of the people so as to create a qualitatively new citizenry, akin to the rest of the societal, economic and political transformations underway. Jose Marti's maxim *"To be educated in order to be free"* has been fully embraced by the Chávez government and his successor, Nicolas Maduro. The raising of people's cultural levels is central to the Bolivarian transformation process. It is so important that the leaders of the Bolivarian process posit that if the revolution is not cultural it is not a revolution.

Venezuela's cultural revolution is strongly influenced by Paulo Freire's pedagogy of the oppressed. It is largely based on the principle that the education process must make the student a protagonist of his/her own education in that "education makes sense because women and men learn that through learning they can make and remake themselves." Thus the creation of a new citizen in the new Venezuela is organized around Freire's dictum:

No pedagogy which is truly liberating can remain distant from the oppressed by treating them as unfortunates and by presenting for their emulation models from among the oppressors. The oppressed must be their own example in the struggle for their redemption. [10]

And those responsible for designing curricula and syllabi make no bones about the nature of what they are seeking to develop: the self-education of the citizenry so that citizens become actors and protagonists of their own liberation. Thus, education policy makers make their objective explicit as though following Freire, whose ethos is aptly summarized by Richard Schaull, author of the Foreword to the 2005, 30th anniversary edition of his acclaimed book *Pedagogy of the Oppressed*:

There is no such thing as a neutral education process. Education either functions as an instrument which is used to facilitate the integration of generations into the logic of the present system and bring about conformity to it, or it becomes the 'practice of freedom', the means by which men and women deal critically with reality and discover how to participate in the transformation of their world. [11]

Thus a system of literature relevant to this objective has been made available, almost totally free of charge, involving the publication and distribution of tens of millions of books, journals, pamphlets, novels, magazines, documentaries, films, music CDs and so forth. This massive intellectual production aims at fomenting a culture of human rights, peace, a pro-environment consciousness, the development of a patriotic and republican mind, rescuing historic memory, strengthening Venezuelan identity, multiculturalism, and the acceptance of diversity. Many of these publications examine the relevance and contemporary validity of the ideas of Simón Rodríguez, Simón Bolívar, and Ezequiel Zamora, among other iconic figures of Venezuela's history.

Bolivarian education stresses the formation of people as social beings seeking to vindicate indigenous and Afro-descendant cultures, thus rejecting the notion of a national identity based on genetic-cultural integration. Art.100 of the Constitution makes this totally explicit:

"The folk cultures comprising the national identity of Venezuela enjoy special attention, with recognition of and respect for intercultural relations under the principle of equality of cultures. Incentives and inducements shall be provided for by law for persons, institutions and communities that promote, support, develop or finance cultural plans, programs and activities within the country and Venezuelan culture abroad. The State guarantees cultural workers inclusion in the Social security system to provide them with a dignified life, recognizing the idiosyncrasies of cultural work, in accordance with law."

The 1999 Bolivarian Constitution enshrines these principles in educational matters and as we will see below they are the motive of specific articles of the fundamental constitutional document of the nation.

The Constitution stipulates that education is a human right and a fundamental social duty; it is democratic, free of charge (up to and including university level) and obligatory, and it is the state's responsibility; it seeks citizens to engage in active, conscious, collective participation in the processes of social transformation; and it is embodied in the values which are part of national identity (Art.102).

Every person has the right to a full, high-quality, ongoing education under conditions of equality, subject only to such limitations as derive from their own aptitudes, and vocational aspirations. The law guarantees equal treatment to persons with special needs or disabilities, and to those who have been deprived of their liberty (Art.103).

Environmental education is obligatory in the various levels and modes of the education system. (Art.107).

Native peoples have the right to preserve and develop their ethnic and cultural identity, their world view, values, spirituality, holy places and places of worship. The State shall promote the appreciation and dissemination of their culture, and native peoples are entitled to an intercultural and bilingual education system that takes into account their special social and cultural characteristics, values and traditions. (Art.121)

To fulfil the objectives of educating the people for them to become protagonists of their own history and emancipation, a free of charge *Sistema Masivo de Revistas* [SMR] (Massive System of Magazines) has been made available.

The SMR consists of 10 magazines: *Asi Somos, A Plena Voz, Arte de Leer, La Roca de Crear, La Revuelta, Poder Vivir, Se Mueve, Memorias de Venezuela*, and the two recent additions, *Buen Vivir* and *Ocho Estrellas*. Each with 64 pages, and 60,000 copies each issue which is feely distributed, and also available on-line free of charge. To this list the magazine *Imagen, Revista Latinoamericana de Cultura*, should be added (a publication of the *Fundacion Editorial El Perro y La Rana*) that contains literary critique, analyses, reviews and in-depth articles on Latin American fiction, theatre, poetry, and popular music (as with the other magazines it is available on line, free of charge). There is also the weekly *Todos Adentro* that should be added to the list (it is a 16-page magazine dedicated to popular culture). And there is the over 300-page *Revista de la Cultura* with scholarly articles and analyses of national cultural developments.

It is to be noted that the magazines that form part of the SMR carry a large number of erudite and scholarly articles on the country's popular traditions such as carnivals and syncretic Afro-Venezuelan and Indigenous festivities, despised and rejected by the dominant Westernised culture of the oligarchy, but respected and celebrated by the poor and the downtrodden. Another strand revisits struggles of workers, peasants, women, and Black slaves who have only been given marginal mention or have simply been ignored in the previous official historiography. Many other magazines concentrate on questioning the previously official identity that deems Venezuelans to be white, Western and Europeanizing, positing instead a reinterpretation of national identity by highlighting the nation's African and Indigenous roots and their manifestations in language, culture, music, dance, customs, food and much more. And, yet another strand of magazines focus on critically analysing that inimitable Latin American genre, the soap opera, but also backward and sexist cultural phenomena such as beauty contests, so important in Venezuelan Westernised culture.

The legitimacy this intense intellectual production gives to the cultural manifestations of the people (as a rule shunned by the less dark-skinned elite and middle class) reverberates among millions of poor Venezuelans. The real nation living under the artificial – previously dominant – Westernised shell is dark-skinned, hard-working, Afro-descendant, indigenous, and whose rich culture is worlds apart from the dominant Caracas-based, Hollywood-like tawdry glamour which has been developed by the country's snobbish yet philistine and shallow Venezuelan oligarchy. In contrast, the culture of the people is rich in traditions, colourfulness, diversity, syncretic religiosity, vibrancy, musicality, dance, folklore, cuisine, legends, and many more fascinating features. Furthermore, because it is based in the struggles of many past generations their culture and identity is rebellious and therefore it embodies the country's history in a way that the dominant one could never possibly do. It is bereft of hypocrisy, is rigged with naughtiness and is picaresque. It is loaded with emancipatory potential. Asi Somos not only rescues the very complex and rich universe of the people of Venezuela, it vindicates them for who they are because of how they are by positively projecting and explaining everything about them. [12] As Venezuelan writer, Luis Britto Garcia, aptly put it: 'We must stop thinking that to be other that what we are is better than being ourselves.'[13]

The wealth of literature (books, journals and pamphlets) that Bolivarian Venezuela produces is rich with historic, sociological, political, ethnographic and anthropological material about Africa's music, customs, uprisings, politics, food, language, games, dance, and many other dimensions of African rich and strong influence on contemporary Venezuela, with an emphasis on explanations about their invisibility in the country's dominant culture. An emblematic intellectual view in this regard is Jesus Chucho Garcia's article 'Demystifying Africa's Absence in Venezuelan History and Culture', whose title captures the new mood about Afro-Venezuelanness.[14]

By way of conclusion

The Bolivarian effort to raise the cultural and intellectual levels of the Venezuelan people is the biggest in that country's history and must rank as one of the biggest such endeavour in Latin America. A similar attempt to educate the population on a mass base was in Allende's Chile where the state publishing house, *Quimantu*, in only 32 months managed to publish a total of 12 million copies of books, pamphlets, and other educational and literary material (more than the total output of Chile's publishing industry in 2002). Upon the ousting of Salvador Allende *Quimantu* was immediately closed down by General Pinochet, and many of its books were burned in public bonfires, and many of its titles were banned during the lengthy 17 years of Pinochet's fascist military dictatorship. Venezuela's *Quimantu* equivalent *Imprenta de la Cultura* had by 2011 printed 95 million copies of books, pamphlets and other educational material, 95% of which is free of charge.

For decades, Venezuela's oligarchy lived off the oil revenues that it pilfered from the nation and kept the bulk of the nation excluded from any social or economic benefits that came about as a result of erratic Hollywoodian modernising impulses.

The stress on national culture, traditions and roots in Venezuelan education is because the salient characteristics of the country's dominant culture is its snobbish acceptance of foreign values and formats whose most grotesque manifestations were weekend shopping sprees in Miami, a heavily *Hollywoodenised* television industry, beauty contests, massive use of plastic surgery, implants and world brand cosmetics, exacerbated obsession with fashion, consumerism, individualism, hedonism, sexism, racism, tackiness, tawdriness, which altogether led to an overrated perception of Hollywood glamour, coupled with contempt for what is viewed as a backward, unsophisticated, local culture. Its corollary has made official Venezuela a rather poor imitation of the 'American way of life'. Caracas epitomises this neurotic syndrome of the Venezuelan oligarchy.

The oligarchy's crucial connection was with the United States. Their privileges, benefits, prestige, enjoyment of the perks of office, lifestyle and everything else that went with it depended totally on the subordination of Venezuela to U.S. strategic and geopolitical considerations on Venezuela's oil. This was the objective reality on which Venezuela's oligarchy's tacky culture rested.

Thus, it is not just exclusion, ignorance, lack of education, poverty, discrimination, exploitation, and so forth that needs to be eradicated, developing the self-esteem of the Venezuelan people entails a massive task. People's minds must be decolonised through their own education.

In the concrete historic circumstances of Venezuela in the 21st century, this could be done only by infusing in them large doses of national pride, which in turn could only be achieved through the positive projection, affirmation and promotion of every aspect associated with the culture of the downtrodden and the history of resistance of the underdog. This is what is being carried out in Venezuela under the Bolivarian government.

However, the chief source of national resources available for such a massive undertaking is the control over the country's oil revenue that the Bolivarian government only managed to obtain only after it wrested the state oil company PDVSA from the

Venezuelan oligarchy after the failure of the oil lockout the Right Wing staged in 2002-2003.[15] Given that the state apparatus of the IV Republic was organised around the private appropriation of the oil by a small retinue of bureaucrats and comprador capitalists, no education of the people on the scale carried out by the Bolivarian government would have been possible.

The Bolivarian national project to educate the people to make them the conscious and educated protagonists of their own destiny is possible because a new state apparatus that responds to the interests of the majority is being built and is being charged with entirely progressive social, political and economic aims, with the mass education of millions of ordinary Venezuelan being central to it. The more the population gets educated along the lines being carried out by the Bolivarian government, the more the people become transformed into the conscious agents of the very transformation underway. The new society being constructed necessitates a new type of citizen.

Footnotes

1   For details see among many others, Fernando Coronil, *The Magical State, Nature, Money and Modernity in Venezuela*, The University of Chicago Press, 1997; Nikolas Kozloff, *Hugo Chavez, Oil, Politics, and the Challenge to the U.S.*, Palgrave Macmillan, 2007; Bart Jones, *Hugo! The Hugo Chavez Story*, Bodley Head, 2008; Richard Gott, *Hugo Chavez and the Bolivarian Revolution*, 2005; and see especially the Liliane Blaser's poignant documentary *Venezuela Febrero 27 (de la Concertacion al Des-Concierto*, 1992); etc.

2   *La Educación Bolivariana Políticas, Programas y Acciones "Cumpliendo Las Metas Del Milenio"*, Ministry of Education and Sports, Caracas 2004, p.25.

3   Francisco Dominguez and Lee Brown, Venezuela: how democracy and social progress are transforming a nation, VSC pamphlet, London, U.K. May 2012, p.17 (this pamphlet can be obtained on line free of charge: http://www.venezuelasolidarity.co.uk/wp-content/uploads/2013/02/vsc-pamphlet-june-2012-free-to-download.pdf

4   ECLAC's special report released in May 2010 (*Time for Equality: closing gaps, opening trails*); UNPD International Human Developments Indicators, Venezuela http://hdrstats.undp.org/en/countries/profiles/VEN.html; Venezuela's Instituto Nacional de Estadisticas can be accessed here http://www.ine.gov.ve/;

5   Cabello: 'El pueblo venezolano puede estar tranquilo, habrá plata para las pensiones", *Correo del Orinoco*, 28 October 2014.

6   A great deal of these data can be found in INDICADORES (http://www.venezueladeverdad.gob.ve/ visited 10 January 2012), but also more up to date figures in *Venezuela en Cifras*, Ministry of Planning, February 2015

7   Mark Weisbrot, Why the US demonises Venezuela's democracy?, *The Guardian*, 3 October 2012.

8   *La Educación Bolivariana Políticas, Programas y Acciones*, op.cit., and Ministerio del Poder Popular para la Planificación: *Venezuela en Cifras*. Venezuela, Febrero 2015, pp. 71-81

9   Data come mainly from Ministerio del Poder Popular para la Planificación: *Venezuela en Cifras*. Venezuela, Febrero 2015, pp. 101-106. The figure for 2014 for TV subscriptions comes from CONATEL, the state radio and TV regulating body (http://www.conatel.gob.ve/venezuela-registra-mas-de-30-millones-de-suscriptores-de-telefonia-movil/).

10 Freire, P. (1970). *Pedagogy of the Oppressed*. New York: Continuum, p.54.

11 Freire, P. (1970). *Pedagogy of the Oppressed*. New York: Continuum, p.34.

12 In an article of mine I suggest that this is widespread phenomenon in Latin America and which is a form of indigenization of politics (see Francisco Dominguez "The Latin Americanization of the Politics of Emancipation" in Lievesey and Ludlam, *Reclaiming Latin America, Experiments in Radical Social Democracy*, Zed Books, 2009, pp.37-54.

13 Luis Britto Garcia, 'Debemos dejar de pensar que ser otros es mejor que ser nosotros mismos", *Asi Somos* 03, June-Dec 2009, p.110

14 Jesus Chucho Garcia' 'Demystifying Africa's Absence in Venezuelan History and Culture", in Sheila S. Walker (ed.), *African Roots / American Cultures, Africa in the Creation of the Americas*, Bowman and Littlefield Publishers Inc., 2001.

15 It must be borne in mind that Venezuela's Right wing in close cahoots with the United States has subjected the Bolivarian government to permanent destabilization since it has tried to overthrow it since its inception in 1999. In this connection see article by Francisco Dominguez, 'Venezuela's Opposition: desperately seeking to overthrow Chavez", in Dominguez, Lievesey and Ludlam (eds) *Right Wing Politics in the New Latin America*, Zed Books, 2011, pp. 113-129.

8 The unexpected crop: social insurgency and new alternatives for education in Mexico

Hugo Aboites

DURING THE year of 2013, Mexico was inundated by massive protests organized by hundreds of thousands of the around 1.5 million teachers that form the mostly public, national school system. 26 of the 32 states of the Republic witnessed some form of protest, for months schools were closed by teachers in several states, the border to the United States was barricaded a couple of days, main national highways were closed for many hours on several occasions and in the City of Mexico tens of thousands of teachers coming from all corners of the country surrounded the National Palace, the building of the Supreme Court, the presidential house, the Stock Market, the City Airport, and made a tent city which occupied for months the main central square of the capital. In this chapter we will try to explain why these protests erupted, what were the dynamics and the tactics of the teachers' movement and what is the present balance. For that we will give first some basic and contextual information.

The national and historical context

The present state Mexican Educational System was created in 1921, a direct result of an armed and bloody revolution (1910-1917) that overthrew a government of landlords, aristocracy and foreign investors. This revolution forced the creation of a national balance of social forces in which poor peasants were given land (a National Land Reform), salaried workers were granted advanced labour rights (Labour Reform), and all children gained access to free public state schools. A national system, funded and administered by the central state, was created to resolve the vast inequalities created by a myriad of small local and very limited systems. For that purpose, the national state established 'normal' schools to educate the children of peasants and workers as teachers. In this manner, nurtured with a socially progressive ideology, these teachers became envoys of a national state which sought to establish a cohesive bond with the revolutionary masses. Later, in 1943, the many regional unions were unified into one single organisation that today has close to 2 million members and that bargains labour conditions and salaries for the vast majority of teachers of the country. The creation of a national union (SNTE), however, put in the hands of the central national state a powerful instrument of control not only of social unrest, but also of the teachers of the country. A large, and very powerful political, social and electoral force was created and for many decades the central state had a high corporative control over the Union. In 1979, however, after a series of previous small movements, a stable opposition force was created within the union (the 'Coordination' or CNTE) and since then it has questioned the control imposed by the state over the union and the corrupt official leadership of the Union that helps maintain it. Given the conditions of existing control, it was quite an achievement that the new Coordination could control around five of the 52 sections that comprised the national union.

A history of neoliberal assaults

The first assault was on salaries. For many years Mexican teachers have been used to finance the expansion of the educational system. Behind the explosive growth of the number of students (which went from less than a million to 20 million in 60 years), is the fact that for almost 40 years (from 1940 onwards) teachers were paid less than what they were making in 1921 (when the national system was created). This meant that for many years, the central government could hire two teachers for the cost of one. It was not only until 1980, forty years later, that the real wages of teachers came back to the level of 1921.

The comeback, however, lasted only a couple of years: in 1982, the real value of salaries suffered once more a reduction of 50 per cent. However this time the unpaid salaries did not go to finance the expansion of the system, but to pay the national external debt, which had gone up astronomically. Up to 70 cents of each Mexican peso of the national budget went to foreign banks. As a response, in the eighties, the opposing teachers joined forces with the newly created faculty unions of universities, and organized a series of strikes during the following years. In 1987 this unrest helped a popular candidate for president who opposed neoliberalism. Because of a clear electoral fraud, he could not win the presidency. However, this led to the creation of a new party, the centre left Party of the Democratic Revolution, which became the third national political force.

In the nineties, a second assault took place in the form of an attempt to decentralize education to the states. This had two objectives: to allow the participation of private interests at the local level and to debilitate the national union. In order to do that, the central government maintained its role but tried to slowly pass on to the local governments the responsibility for the annual bargaining process. The teachers, however every year built a movement that forced the central government to maintain national negotiations and, at the same time, successfully used local bargaining to obtain additional gains. This double game empowered the teacher movements both at the national and local level. Twenty years later, in 2013, the central government finally gave up and decided again to centralise the education system, but teachers nevertheless continue successfully win improvements in local negotiations.

A third neoliberal assault on Mexican teachers came in 2008 with the government initiative to introduce a series of changes in education under the name of Alliance for Quality Education (ACE)in association with some of the national biggest economic interests. Among other things, the initiative aimed at establishing evaluation of teachers, changing the rules for joining the education service and increasing the participation of businessmen in local schools. Strengthened by years of collective actions at the local level, teachers reacted promptly and massively. Union sections that were in the hands of a corrupt leadership subordinated to the central government revolted and took the buildings of the local sections, threw away the old bosses, and appointed new democratic leaders. So, the strength of the teachers' movement increased substantially with tens of thousands of new converted teachers. The Alliance succeeded in some points (such as changing the rules for joining the service), but helped to create a wider base of organized opposition.

In 2012 the centre-right party (PAN) proposed a legislation which would establish a periodical "universal evaluation", that is, for each one of the almost two million teachers. Eventually, many teachers could be fired. The fortified teachers movement, however, responded quickly, surrounded the National Congress buildings, and pressured for negotiations. The differences of opinion of legislators on how to carry out an overall reform of education was a decisive help to the teachers' movement. Lacking a previous and detailed agreement, they were faced with arguments to which they did not have coherent and consistent answers. They lacked a comprehensive vision of exactly what reform they wanted. That led to contradictions and sometimes an open and angry debate right there in front of the teachers' negotiation team. These circumstances obliged parties to opt for retreat and the legal initiative was cancelled. But not for long.

At the end of 2013 a new president of the Republic was elected and appointed. Behind curtains and months before, he had convinced the three main parties – including the leftist Party of the Democratic Revolution (PRD) – to agree on a national agenda of constitutional and legal changes which consisted mainly on an overall reform of the labour conditions of teachers. Excluding them from the national labour relations framework established by the constitution (which would never allow the dismissal of a teacher as the result of an evaluation, nor for the establishment of sanctions in the hands of educational authorities for any reason they may think of), they sought to defuse the strengthening process of the teachers' movement, and to subordinate teachers to a condition of vulnerability that no other sector of workers had. They were able to carry on and approve what was called the Educational Reform, which involved nothing less than changing the constitution, in order to consolidate changes at the maximum level of the national norms. The result was a monumental rebellion that included many more sections of the national union and actions not seen before in a century of labour movements, as described at the beginning of this piece. After the constitutional change, and in the middle of the protests, came the approval of what were called the secondary laws, which specified down to details the significance of the constitutional change.

In spite of its force, the movement was not able to stop the legal changes (with the exception of only a few cosmetic alterations) but achieved other important political gains. For example, at the beginning of 2013 it was clear that the teachers' movement was no longer a confined and isolated small group of union sections but a national current involving hundreds of thousands of teachers and tens of sections.

The political strategy designed by the national assembly of teachers and some other popular organisations, on the other hand, lead to a clear moral and political victory for the movement. The tour of a handful of academics that covered every corner of a country inhabited by more than one hundred million gave teachers an advanced and well-founded critical view of the reform. It was an authoritarian process imposed by the president in complicity with the leadership of three parties, with no room for discussion (it took Congress less than ten days to modify the constitution, a process that normally takes months of debates, and many of the legislators did not even had a chance to read the proposed changes, but voted in favour anyway). It was also a so called reform of education that was never even founded on a minimal diagnosis of the situation of education and a clear argument on how these types of changes will contribute to the betterment of schools. In fact it was proven that more than an education reform it was a labour one. Its main thrust was to alter the labour conditions of teachers and subordinate them. Furthermore, it created a state of exception, only for teachers of public schools. Those of private schools would be evaluated, but could not be fired. It also created a climate of rigid control and supervision in the classrooms and schools as teachers were even going to be videotaped to register if and how they complied with standards of teaching conduct. Finally it was demonstrated with public documents that the basic blueprint of the reforms had been drawn up months before it was proposed to the Congress by a research centre of the most powerful firms of the country (including Coca-Cola, beer companies, the main TV chain, etc.). It was a big business reform of education.

The victory in the battle of the arguments had a strong impact on the media. Although many of the newscasts, newspapers and other media severely criticized teachers, calling them "vandals", "lazy", the internet and other very respected and independent media chose to criticize the government and legislators because they hadn't given teachers and civil organizations a chance to engage in a real dialogue on the reform. It was a fast track reform.

Also, teachers argued that the reform would contribute to the privatization of schools. At first it was not clear how this would happen, but and the government helped to prove the point when, based on a few phrases of the reform text that spoke of promoting the autonomy of schools, middle level officials started to notify schools that as a result of the reform now they would have to pay the electricity, water and telephone bills, as a way to become independent. The amount to pay was astronomically high for many poor parents who were in fact already helping to provide schools with blackboards, bathrooms, running water..Infuriated, parents starting the occupy schools and close them down, sometimes in spite of teachers who would not dare to paralyse them as part of the protest.

Most importantly, the whole movement and its arguments had a clear impact on the legitimacy of the reform. A year later, it has yet to produce an impact on the change and betterment of educational processes and schools and it is met with scepticism and lethargy by the local governments. So much so that the central government is now suing in the Supreme Court some states that have not adequately changed their local laws to the tune of the national legislation. Teachers confront local governments at every move they make to try to impose the law.

A law that has no support from those in charge of complying with it, is almost a dead law. Especially in the field of education, forcing a law to be accepted is even more difficult given that it requires the agreement of almost two million persons who devote their life to knowledge. It is harder to convince them of the value of something that mistreats them, and the impact of what they think is very powerful in the communities. Two million teachers unconvinced and hundreds of thousands openly and with good reasons against it, is a very powerful force.

The unexpected crop

The most interesting part of this process of assault-resistance is the important change that has been happening in the vision of teachers. In 1979, when the Coordination started, the motto was "salary and democracy" the latter referring to the need to get rid of the oppressive union leadership. But by 2008 it was clear that the focus had undergone an important change. Yes, it still was salary and democracy but it also included the defence of the right of teachers to begin changing education by themselves. Teachers escaped from pure trade unionism and moved into the discussion and practice of new alternatives for education. First in 2008, with the Alliance for Quality Education described above, the rebel teachers not only took the union buildings that had been in the hands of corrupt leaders for more than sixty years, they also started to take education in their own hands. They perceived that it was not only the conditions in which they work that were at stake with this type of reform, but also the foundation itself of the education they had been prepared to create as part of the new nation emerged from the 1910-1917 Revolution. The popular, critical and national vision of education was giving way to a business orientation. That meant an emphasis on "quality", "competencies", "merit", "ranking", and created an atmosphere in which they, the poor and their students will be persecuted or marginalised. So, coupled with the demonstrations and marches teachers in several states organized "congresses" as they were called, which reunited hundreds of parents, in one occasion; large numbers of students in another; also communities and parents. From all this, new proposals for education started to emerge.

This lead to a re-appreciation of many projects organized by teachers and communities founded years before. In these projects, prehispanic languages were rescued as well as the culture they belong to in what is a very plural country, with more than sixty different original languages. Teachers and communities also organized projects of production and services to benefit students and the whole community. In some states, like Oaxaca, Guerrero, Michoacán, fully-fledged alternative schools were created, and all the schools of the state rejected standardised testing.

At the same time, in 2008, in the state of Chiapas, the Zapatista armed rebellion had not only achieved a form of relative autonomy but also managed to create a whole education system as a way to substitute for the government schools. It goes from elementary to middle school and then to the university level, with the so called University of the Land. This alternate system has a very different curricula, of course, and the teachers are trained youngsters from the original peoples communities.

The winds of reform have reached the cities also. Since the middle of the nineties, student movements have grown against national standardised testing and in protest at the scarcity of spaces in higher education (Mexico has one of the lowest levels of coverage in Latin America). These reached a peak in 1999-2000 when the National University (home of 300 hundred thousand students) was closed for nine months by the student movement. They protested against increased tuition fees, standardised testing and time limits to complete studies, and demanded wider student participation in institutional decisions. As a result of these and other movements the pressure for change mounted, and eventually the local government, opposing the national neoliberal education policies, created a new type of university, the Mexico City Autonomous University – public, financed by the City and the federal government, free of any tuition costs, with no admission exam, no time limit to finish the studies, and governed by a council of students and faculty. It is specially dedicated to research, the diffusion of knowledge and the promotion of cultural expressions throughout the city. Faculty teach at the five campuses of the institution but also at five different correctional facilities, and it's starting a program which will create 16 cultural and learning centres in low income areas, run by students and faculty.

Students are very active politically and they have defended their university against hostile government initiatives to change the fundamental law of the institution and turn it into a regular boring, expensive and elitist university.

In these many ways, educational reforms have been counteracted by the creativity, initiative and strength of the popular and teachers' movements.

9 From Resistance to Renewal: the emergence of social movement unionism in England

Gawain Little & Howard Stevenson

FOR MANY YEARS, education policy in England has been at the forefront of what has become known as the Global Education Reform Movement.[1] Alongside Chile and parts of the United States, England has appeared as a vanguard movement in terms of the neoliberal reform and restructuring of state education[2]. The focus on England is important, because within the United Kingdom education policy is devolved to individual nations and different policy trajectories between, for example, England and Scotland, are stark. English education policy has taken a particularly distinctive turn, and this has had profound effects on relations with teachers as an occupational group, and on teachers organised in their unions in particular.

Relationships between teacher unions and the state have provided a key focus for the reforms of the English education system. This is partly because teacher unions are presented as an obstacle to many of the key reforms such as vastly increased private sector involvement in public education. However organised teachers are more directly a target of the reforms for other reasons. Firstly, teachers' pay is a significant cost to government and a neoliberal commitment to 'small government' dictates a constant need to contain payroll costs. Secondly, teachers are a strategically important group of workers who perform a critical ideological function. If the education system is to be subordinated further to meeting the needs of capital, it is essential that there is greater control over the curriculum, and hence teachers' work. In England this control is being achieved through a combination of market forces and state-driven managerialism[3]. Attacking the power and influence of teacher unions, as the collective representation of the teaching profession, is therefore both a policy end in itself, and a means to an end.

The scale of the attacks on organised teachers are considerable but should be seen as part of a longer-term project. Over time, centralised national collective bargaining has been replaced by fragmentation, including individualised pay and increasing contract flexibility. Traditional union structures and ways of organising now seem out of kilter with this new landscape.

English teacher unionism is characterised by a complex multi-unionism[4] in which at least six different unions compete for members amongst different, but often overlapping, sectors of the school workforce.

In this chapter we focus on how the largest teachers' union in England, the National Union of Teachers (NUT) is responding to these changes. In particular, we identify the emergence of an embryonic form of social movement unionism,[5] characterised by grassroots organising, community coalition building and mobilisation around an alternative vision of education.

The neoliberal assault

The background to the neoliberal assault on English schools lies in the economic debates of the 1970s [6], the 'discourse of derision' about education that developed from 1976 [7] and the 'Black papers' of 1969 onwards [8] but the defining moment was 1988.

The 1988 Education Reform Act introduced a number of market measures into the education system, including 'choice' and competition, local management of schools, per-capita funding, standardised testing and the introduction of City Technology Colleges and Grant Maintained Schools. At the same time, it increased central control by the department through measures such as a standardised curriculum and the introduction of 'Key Stages' with a number of specific objectives to be achieved at each stage.

The explicit intention of this was increased market competition. Education Secretary Kenneth Baker set this out for the North of England Conference in 1988 when he said, 'Parents should not have to accept second best within a local authority monopoly of free education. If the product is not all it should be, parents should not be put in the position of having to like it or lump it'.[9]

Every school would be responsible for its own budget and the funding formula would be based on the number of 'customers' it could attract. As Margaret Thatcher declared, the intention was that 'money will flow to the good schools and good headmasters' (sic)[10].

However, in spite of the significance of the changes introduced by the 1988 Act, it stopped short of full privatisation. As educationalist Brian Simon wrote in 1987, the Education Reform Act comprised 'a subtle set of linked measures are to be relied upon to have the desired effect – that is to push the whole system towards a degree at least, of privatisation, establishing a base which could be further exploited later'.[11]

This 'subtle set of linked measures' changed the nature of education fundamentally and, in spite of different emphases, the fundamental direction of travel has not been challenged by any successive government. Indeed, it is arguably the New Labour Governments from 1997 - 2010, with the creation of Academies (state-funded independent schools) and further undermining of local authorities, that created the platform on which the past five years' race to achieve the '1988 project' [12] occurred.

Since the election of the coalition government in 2010, the pace of the project has once again picked up, starting with the introduction of the Academies Act in 2010. This act streamlined the process for schools to convert into academies and introduced the concept of 'free' schools, at the same time restricting the right of local authorities to open new schools.

In May 2010, there were just 203 academies. By January 2015, this had leapt to 4404, representing 13% of primary schools and 55% of secondary schools. The right-wing Conservative Government elected in May 2015 has committed in its manifesto to 'turn every failing and coasting secondary school into an academy"and to give all 'good"schools (including academies, 'free' schools and selective grammar schools) the right to expand.

In 2012 the government removed the requirement for academies and 'free' schools to employ qualified teachers.

Alongside the fragmentation of the education system and the deregulation of teaching, the government also mounted direct attacks on teachers' pay and conditions.

In 2010, they embarked on a review of public sector pensions, with the intention that: *"The new pensions will be substantially more affordable to alternative providers... we are no longer requiring private, voluntary and social enterprise providers to take on the risks of defined benefit that deter many from bidding for contracts in the first place."*

(Danny Alexander, Chief Secretary to the Treasury, 2011)[13]

In 2013, via the supposedly independent School Teachers' Review Body (STRB), the government abolished the national pay structure for teachers, effectively introducing institution-level bargaining, whilst stipulating that pay must be directly linked to 'performance' and student results.

Most recently, the government has introduced a 'baseline' test for 4-year olds to be taken within the first six weeks of school. The test will be mandatory from 2016 and schools have a choice of six approved private providers to purchase the assessment from. The government has been clear that the purpose of this test will be to judge the effectiveness of schools and teachers.

These changes represent a fundamental reshaping of school sector labour relations in England. Until the mid-1980s teacher unions enjoyed considerable influence in a world where national collective bargaining was dominant, and teacher union influence at local authority level was also considerable. Union organisation tended to mirror this centralised structure in which national and local authority level negotiations established the framework in which teachers performed their work in schools. School level union organisation was minimal as key bargaining and decision-making structures operated at higher levels in the system.

With the abolition of national pay scales in 2013 and the increasing fragmentation of the system via the academy programme, the school, or the academy chain, is increasingly the principal bargaining unit.

Pathways of resistance

When the Conservative-led coalition came to power in May 2010, the NUT was already engaged in a joint boycott of standardised tests for 11 year olds, alongside the National Association of Head Teachers. Around 1 in 4 schools participated which, whilst not enough to defeat the tests themselves, did call into question the accuracy of league tables and help build deeper opposition to testing amongst teachers, parents and the wider public.

Following the election, the Union was immediately in battles over cuts to school funding, the Academies Bill and public sector pension cuts. They began a long campaign amongst the membership on the latter, including encouraging members to write to their MP, joint material produced with other teacher unions and a 'pensions roadshow'. At the end of February, after nine months of campaigning, the Union started warning members to 'be prepared to vote for industrial action to protect your pension'.

In April, delegates at the NUT Annual Conference in Harrogate voted overwhelmingly to ballot for strike action and the ballot ran from mid-May to mid-June. The Union received a positive result and announced a day of joint action on 30th June with education union ATL, civil servants union PCS and university union UCU.

At the same time that the Union took strike action over the attack on public sector pensions, and maintained a clear focus within that on teachers' pensions [14], it launched a national petition *Fair Pensions for All* which also called for an increase in the state pension and for employers to be obliged to offer decent occupational pensions. This shows an attempt to reach out beyond the NUT and the public sector, but balanced with an attempt to engage members on the question of 'their' pension.

This showed in the slogans on the day: *Save Our Pensions* and Fair Pensions for All. The difference in narratives is clear here and represents a contradiction which was not just inherent in the NUT's campaign but to a greater extent in that of a number of other unions.

The action on 30th June was followed by a number of discussions amongst the public sector unions about ballots and further dates and, at the Trade Union Congress on 14th September 2011, General Secretary after General Secretary took to the stage to announce that their union would be balloting for, or taking, action on 30th November.

The build up to 30th November was unprecedented. On the day, 30 unions took action, bringing out around 2 million public sector workers. This was the biggest strike in Britain since the 1926 General Strike and the biggest strike of women in British history.

In the months preceding the action, local trade union branches worked within Trades Councils and alongside local anti-cuts campaigns that had sprung up over the previous two years to co-ordinate local support networks to get out the vote and the strike, and to plan marches and demonstrations for the day. Unions leafleted each other's workplaces.

This brought many NUT activists into contact with a wider section of the trade union movement and the political left than they had been in contact with previously and developed strong bonds of solidarity. It also gave many new activists a taste of working inside a broader movement, and one with considerable energy and focus.

However, one of the strengths of the 'Great Pensions Strike' was also one of its greatest weaknesses. The day of action had spontaneously brought together a number of unions who were all faced with the same challenge but were approaching it from a number of different perspectives.

Whilst some were trying to emphasise the direct link to privatisation and calling for further co-ordinated action and the extension of this to the political sphere, several unions viewed the strike purely or primarily as an opportunity to improve their bargaining position in negotiations. They began to engage in scheme specific talks over 'Heads of Agreement' and to discuss proposals which they eventually persuaded their members to accept without further action.[15]

The November 2011 strike won some concessions from government. For teachers this amounted to an improvement of about £800 per year of retirement and exemption for those aged 50 and over from the plans. Never-the-less the main issue of cutting the value of pensions in order to further privatisation of public services was not tackled head on.

The real gains of the strike lay mainly in the fact that it brought a generation of activists to see the potential power that workers and their unions can wield when fighting alongside a broader alliance of activists and, for teachers, the impact of all the major teaching unions overcoming their historic division and acting together.

March 2012 saw the NUT take one further day of regional strike action in London alongside the UCU but with the vast majority of unions having taken their members out of the fight, it was clear that another strategy was needed.

On 28th May 2012, NUT and NASUWT, the two largest teaching unions, announced an 'historic' partnership.[16] The NUT conducted a further ballot to widen the issues of its original dispute and on 3rd October began action short of strike action jointly with NASUWT.

This action was different, both in terms of its content and the way in which it had been developed. On 29th May, at a national meeting of local association secretaries, workshops were held to discuss what form the non-strike action should take and which non-strike sanctions would be most effective in relieving the burden of excessive workload in schools. This direct engagement of local activists was crucial to developing action which chimed directly with local experience and which had a level of local buy-in even before it was launched.

The guidance consisted of 25 instructions (expanded to 26 in winter 2013)[17] which would give NUT members, and crucially school groups, the authorisation to implement any action or combination of actions that they felt would make a difference to workload and morale in their school.

This was a difficult step, as it meant the union nationally had less control over how, and when, the action took place. It also meant a lot of work had to go into popularising the action in local areas and in individual schools. However, by its very nature, it put school groups and workplace reps in the driving seat. It also gave significant incentive for local secretaries to visit schools, meet with school groups and support them in taking collective decisions over action at school level.

2013 was dominated by the decision of the School Teachers' Review Body (STRB), the 'independent' body which has reviewed teachers' pay and conditions annually since the abolition of collective bargaining, to agree the Secretary of State's recommendations on deregulating teachers' pay.

The NUT and NASUWT responded by calling rolling regional strikes in June and October. These strikes were well supported and, with the two largest teachers' unions working together, had a significant impact in terms of school closures. When the STRB released its report early the following year, refusing Michael Gove's request to abolish whole sections of the School Teachers' Pay and Conditions Document, the strikes were credited with encouraging this unprecedented slap in the face for the Secretary of State. Among the conditions Gove sought to remove were the right to a lunch break, 10% planning preparation and assessment time, and limits on the number of days and hours a year teachers can be directed to work.

It was at these regional strikes that green T-shirts began to appear, bearing the slogan *Stand Up for Education*. These T-shirts were produced and spread across the country by rank and file union activists and *Stand Up for Education* became the unofficial slogan of the strikes.

Following the October strikes, a planned one-day strike by both unions failed to materialise. Officially, this was because Michael Gove had agreed to talks (and indeed a series of talks did begin later that year). However, it was clear to any observer that there was growing friction within the 'historic' partnership. This became public when NUT announced further strike action on 26th March 2014, only to be followed by the news that NASUWT would not be taking action.

It is here that the story takes an interesting turn. At the end of February 2014, with the prospect of taking action alone after two years of joint action with other teaching unions, the NUT took a strategic decision to reorient its campaign to a wider audience. In the face of being isolated within the teaching unions, NUT turned to the parents and others who had expressed so much support for the campaign so far.

This looks like a rather sudden decision but in reality is was the culmination of months of discussion on the Union's National Executive and amongst grassroots activists. It built upon an orientation towards parents and the wider community which has been present, though not so explicit, in the NUT's work for decades and on discussions that were taking place internally about the future of the union.

In early March, the Union adopted the *Stand Up for Education* slogan as the official slogan of the campaign and began to reorient its approach, bringing a number of issues to the fore which had been key to its arguments but not fully elaborated previously. In particular, the initial Stand Up for Education leaflets and petition had five central demands which linked the neoliberal attack on education directly to children's experience of education and teachers' working conditions.

The Union developed a campaign strategy of Engage (parents and the wider community), Pressure (the politicians) and Strike (for education).

Engagement with parents and the wider community necessitated a re-engagement with the union's own activists. Up and down the country, weekly street stalls took place, as well as cake sales, coffee mornings and other activities. Members shared successes on Twitter and Facebook and a real energy was developed around the campaign.

The 26th March strike took place in the early phase of this development and was enthused by the energy of the new direction. At meetings of the National Executive, a number of areas reported increased engagement in spite of the loss of a key ally.

In many ways, the breakdown of the alliance with the NASUWT, whilst regrettable, allowed the NUT to develop a much more creative, broad and deep campaign. Many NUT activists gained experience of taking the arguments out more broadly and a new layer of members were encouraged into union activity.

This activity continued until the summer, with some local associations sustaining weekly community events and activities from the beginning of March right the way through to the end of the academic year in July. The second prong of the strategy was developed through targeted email campaigns and local lobbies of MPs, as well as a national lobby on 10th June.

This was followed at the end of June by a mass NUT presence on the national march called by the People's Assembly Against Austerity. Several thousand teachers made a sea of green as they marched in their *Stand Up for Education* T-shirts. One of the most interesting aspects of this was that it was not primarily driven by a central mobilisation of the national union. As one National Executive member commented after the demonstration, 'the interesting thing is that they were not there as a result of exhortations from NUT HQ but because they have been engaged with union activity, running stalls, pressuring politicians etc and through that activity see the importance of being part of the wider movement.'[18]

On 10th of July, the NUT took a further day of national strike action, this time alongside Unite, Unison and GMB. The Department for Education put out a press release in which they claimed that the strike would, "achieve nothing and benefit no-one".[19] Five days later, Michael Gove was removed as Education Secretary.

By the end of the year, the new Secretary of State had launched a 'Workload Challenge' to which 44,000 teachers responded, telling the government what the main causes of excessive workload are and what can be done to address them. To date, government has failed to give any meaningful response to this consultation. However, it has contributed considerably to shifting the debate around teaching and education.

In the run up to the general election in May 2015, the NUT produced a *Stand Up for Education* manifesto for education. Over three million copies were produced and distributed and it was endorsed by hundreds of public figures from children's authors, to academics, to parliamentary candidates.

The manifesto was used for a range of local activism in addition to street stalls and lobbies of candidates. Crucial to this were Education Question Times, where the public could question politicians, union activists, academics and educationalists. They provided a space for teachers, parents and community activists to articulate their views on education and confront their parliamentary candidates.

In spite of the outcome of the general election, which was narrowly won by the right-wing Tory party, this work has helped to develop wider networks around the union and to begin to elaborate the progressive alternative.

Green shoots of renewal

Behind the story of teacher resistance over the past five years lies a deeper transformation. We argue that there that this is composed of three main elements: a shift to a grassroots organising approach, an increasing focus on alliances and the wider community, and a political approach which challenges neoliberalism and seeks to build around an alternative vision for education. We further argue that, taken together, these changes constitute the emergence of an embryonic form of 'social movement unionism' and that this social movement unionism has the potential to pose a real threat to the neoliberal consensus.

A central argument within this chapter is that the labour relations framework that existed for many years in England is now barely recognisable. This opens up huge questions for teacher unions about how they react, both in terms of their campaigning stance and their conduct of industrial relations with employers. Teacher unions need a coherent strategy which responds to both sides of this dilemma – the industrial and the political/educational.

Our approach here is to draw on a framework developed by Carter et al. (2010) in an earlier study of labour relations in the English education system, which identifies three possible responses to reform – *rapprochement, resistance and renewal*. We use this framework as a useful starting point for analysis, whilst recognising that the change in context since 2010 necessitates some redefining of the terms.

Rapprochement can be considered to be a pragmatic 'coming to terms' with the direction of neoliberal restructuring, and an attempt within those parameters to develop arrangements for consultation and negotiation that maximise the benefits to union members. This approach does not necessarily accept the logic of policy reform but it does, pragmatically, go with the grain of policy when seeking to further the interests of members.

Resistance describes the situation where teacher unions seek to actively challenge the trajectory of policy and explicitly reject its neoliberal dimensions, often through industrial action. Such an approach was identified by Carter et al. in the 2010 study, and largely associated with the NUT during that time (as the main union that remained outside of 'social partnership' with the New Labour government). Whilst the approach had some successes, it also suffered from two weaknesses. First, despite its commitment to activism it paradoxically continued to assume a largely passive membership. There was little understanding of how, or under what specific circumstances, members might respond to calls for industrial action. Second, the approach remained dependent on a small number of 'hero-activists', undertaking disproportionate amounts of union work. The frailties of this model have become increasingly clear.

The *union renewal* thesis [20] shares many elements of the strategy of resistance identified above, notably a rejection of neoliberal reform and a commitment to challenge this through mobilising collective action. However, the union renewal thesis goes further by recognising the need for unions to adapt their own form and organisation. There is a recognition that decentralised decision-making (even when highly centralised elements still remain) requires unions to adapt their structures in ways that mirror this. Fairbrother's [21] analysis recognises there is some element of threat from these developments (with employee isolation undermining traditional solidarities), but he also argues that the emergence of new bargaining issues at the workplace represented an opportunity to draw union members into engagement with the union. Renewal would follow when increased rank and file participation rejuvenated what could sometimes be moribund and bureaucratic union structures. The extent to which this might happen would depend in large part on the extent to which the union restructured in order to encourage this rank and file participation. This is precisely the process of restructuring that the NUT has begun to engage in.

As has been argued above, historically the NUT's priorities have been the maintenance of a local authority based school system, and ultimately a return to national collective bargaining. As long as these goals seemed like possibilities in the short to medium term, arguably it made sense to retain union structures and ways of organising that reflected these objectives. However, before very long into the life of the Coalition government it became palpably clear that traditional ways of doing things were no longer fit for purpose. The kind of resistance the union was mounting relied on a massive increase in member activism at all levels, something the old structures were not able to deliver.

From 2010 onwards, a political and cultural shift began to take place in the union as activists and officers across the NUT began to face up to the scale of the changes taking place, and the potential implications for the future (or not) of the union itself.

Organising

'Organising is about helping working people to build power and agency [through] increasing their strength in the workplace" (White, 2013).

Evidence of the union's commitment to an organising strategy had already begun to emerge long before the election of the Coalition government in 2010. For example, in August 2009 the union appointed a Head of Organising post at a senior level [22], and by 2011 the union had a team of 11 organisers working in the regions across the country. The job of a local organiser was a new role in the union as previously full time union officials in the regions were focused on supporting branches with their negotiations amd undertaking considerable amounts of individual casework. In contrast, the role of union organisers was to work with local branches to build local union capacity. Their focus therefore was principally on strengthening the local lay structures through recruiting and supporting school-based union representatives. In 2013 the union appointed 20 organisers, many on fixed term contracts, but by 2014 this team had grown to 32 organisers, overwhelmingly in permanent positions.

Whilst a formal evaluation of the project has not yet been carried out, by 2014 the union was able to report a 60% increase in the number of workplace representatives and a 250% increase in the number of trained representatives.[23]

Training for representatives has undergone a thorough revision to reflect both their new role in the workplace and the union's turn to organising. The new foundation course is heavily based on John Kelly's work on Mobilisation Theory:

From the vantage point of mobilization theory it is the perception of, and response to, injustice that should form the core intellectual agenda for industrial relations... Whilst the roots of collective interest definition lie in perceived injustice, it is crucial that workers attribute their problems to an agency which can be held responsible either for causing their problem or ameliorating it (or both). Normally this agency would be the employer, although it might also be the state. Such attributions of blame both derive from and reinforce a sense of distinct group identity...[24]

Kelly points to the importance of "a small but critical mass of activists" whose role involves "promoting a sense of grievance" by challenging accepted inequalities and creating or sustaining "a high degree of group cohesion".[25]

What is particularly exciting about this approach is that it assumes not just a high degree of agency on the part of union activists but also a recognition of their explicitly political role in challenging inequality in order to promote collective action.

This approach runs throughout much of the union's work and is probably best exemplified in the definition of leadership given by Deputy General Secretary Kevin Courtney (see below).

Leadership

School, college and other workplace reps provide the key layer of leadership in an organising union like the NUT.

Historically the national Union conducted negotiations with central government on a wide range of subjects. Agreements reached were then binding on all schools. The Union's divisions, which correspond to local authorities, replicated this process over matters that were decided at this level.

In that context a narrow view of what leadership needs to be in a union could develop. A skilled negotiator could 'win' for all teachers and those teachers did not 'need' to be involved in their union. For many years the overall political climate was such that teachers did not 'need' community support to win.

But now, all that has changed. Decisions are increasingly made at school or college level – whether in academies or community schools and colleges. Our opponents seek a wide-ranging counter reform in education.

Exclusively top down leadership will not work.
Leadership must now also be local, upward and outward.

- Victories are now won and setbacks recorded at all levels; school/college, local authority and national. We need democratic and effective leadership in all these layers of the Union.

- Membership involvement makes all the difference. The leadership layer that interacts with those members, and can inspire them, must become increasingly important in our Union.

- Victories or defeats in one workplace can spread to others – so a rep that can talk to and influence other reps around them is playing a vital leadership role.

- Our local and national union structures will best understand the issues and respond to them when local leaders can give leadership upwards.

- Our opponents seek a wide ranging counter reform in education. NUT groups with strong links outwards, to parents and the wider community, are vital in resisting that.

Your role as a local leader of the NUT is critical
in the fight for education and teachers.

Kevin Courtney
NUT Deputy General Secretary

Following a 2014 training session for workplace representatives in academy chains, one participant described it this way:

Was this the day that the union was given back to the membership? Well, it felt like that to me.

It's clear that the traditional ways of bargaining at a national and local authority level are changing. What replaces it is on the one hand quite ominous, but also quite empowering.

Increasingly in the future it will be down to union members to organise themselves and take up the cause at school and academy-chain level, as well as within local authorities.

As a consequence, the union has to adapt and this is all about engaging reps and members on the issues that are most pressing.

The days of waiting for 'the union' to do it for us are disappearing fast. I left the day having made some firm connections with colleagues and feeling that what I always wanted to be true had been reaffirmed – the union belongs to the members and it's the members who will determine what happens next.[26]

Community unionism

The second main transformation to take place within the NUT is an increasing orientation to parents and to working people more generally. The neoliberal attack on education does not just affect terms and conditions, it affects teachers' entire professional lives. Beyond that, it affects everyone associated with schools and education. And because schools lie at the heart of their communities, it affects everyone within that community.

In this sense, the global assault on education affects all working people. Therefore, opposition to it has the potential to mobilise all working people in response. Schools, at the heart of their communities, provide a focal point of that opposition. However, for this potential to be realised, teacher unions need to broaden their focus and work to link their activism to the wider concerns of parents and others.

As Amanda Tattersall argues:

When unions… enter into strong, reciprocal and agenda-setting coalitions, the labor movement increases its chances of building a new political climate while winning on major issues that they have been losing. More mutual and shared relationships among unions and community organisations can also help revitalize unions internally, invigorating their political vision, campaign techniques, and membership engagement…

Coalitions are a source of power for unions, not simply because they supplement a union's objectives with the resources of another organisation but because they help renew unions. This kind of strength requires a sometimes challenging kind of reciprocal coalition building. Yet this slower, stronger coalition practice can help unions rebuild their internal capacity, develop new leaders, and innovate how they campaign. Coalitions can also shift unions from being agents focused on the workplace to becoming organizations that connect workplace concerns with a broad agenda that in turn can transform the broader political climate. As

Flanders (1970) expressed it, coalitions allow unions to act not only in their "vested interests" but with a "sword of justice".[27]

One of the most fundamental shifts in the NUT's campaigning was the decision in March 2014, just weeks before a national strike, to launch the *Stand Up for Education* campaign. This campaign explicitly focuses on educational issues and situates the union's industrial concerns within this context. By putting students and their education at the centre of the campaign, the union has challenged the accusations of its critics that teachers are only interested in their own terms and conditions. At the same time, it has reached out to the wide base of nascent support that exists amongst parents and communities for progressive educational advance.

The recognition that teachers cannot win alone is crucial, and the connection of educational issues to wider societal issues, such as child poverty is both necessary and an important opportunity to widen the political perspectives on NUT activists themselves. In the aftermath of the 2015 General Election, many on the left are asking how it will be possible to rebuild a progressive alternative given how deeply embedded reactionary control of the media and public opinion are in British culture. Building political engagement around concrete issues, based on a politically-aware core of activists must be a key part of the answer and this is the potential that this path of community engagement offers.

However, this is probably the least-developed strand of the NUT's work and is still largely driven by the union, which has set out its policies and begun to mobilise around them. This is an inevitable starting point but it is to be hoped that this can develop into a genuine dialogue in which parents are engaged as equals in defining the future of their children's education.

When we talk about engaging parents and the wider community in the Stand Up for Education campaign, this is not just about building temporary alliances but about sustainable coalitions within a broader movement on education. It should change our unions as much as it changes the context within which they operate.
(Courtney & Little, 2014)

An alternative vision

One of the key aims of the Stand Up for Education campaign is to begin to articulate an alternative to the neoliberal orthodoxy that has dominated education for the last thirty years or more. This domination has not been achieved purely, or even primarily, through political confrontation with those advocating progressive education but through defining the very terms of the debate itself.[28]

This constitutes hegemony, the term used by Antonio Gramsci to describe the dominance achieved by a social group by means of consent or 'intellectual and moral leadership'.[29] As John Hoffman [30] argues, this consent never exists in pure form but always in a relationship with coercion – "coercion which commands consent". Part of this process of building hegemony involves the creation of a narrative, in this case around education, which prescribes the limits of debate. Some questions are explicitly or implicitly ruled out of order and those who step outside of the dominant narrative can expect either to be discounted for being outside of the consensus or to be disciplined via the mechanisms of coercion which reinforce consent.[31] In the case of education, OFSTED has played a particularly crucial role in reinforcing neoliberal hegemony.

Analysing the discourse of the New Right through the 1980s, Stephen Ball writes of the 'setting of expertise against commonsense. The role of expert knowledge and research is regarded as less dependable than political intuition and commonsense accounts of what people want'.[32] This is recognisable in the discourse of neoliberal reform in the last five years, from Michael Gove's denunciation of 'the Blob'[33] to his declaration that 'what's right is what works"in the context of a heavily ideological speech backed up with little material evidence.[34]

Following Kenway[35], Ball argues that 'the effectiveness of such polarities is related both to the divisions they generate – parents against teachers, scholarly research against the popular media – and the unities they conjure up – parents as a group, of a kind, teachers as a group, of a kind. The interests of all parents are cast together as the same. 'Disparate and contradictory interests [are] activated and welded into a common position' (Kenway, 1987 p43)'.[36] This, then, is hegemony in action.

In order to challenge this dominant discourse, teacher unions need to begin to articulate an alternative vision of education and to win people to it by linking broad policy aspirations to their lived daily experience.[37]

The NUT has explicitly made it part of its aim to begin to articulate such a vision and to build a movement around it which is capable of challenging neoliberalism. This thread runs through initiatives such as the development of the *Stand Up for Education* manifesto and the *Fighting for Education* strategy document which accompanied it. It also runs through union training for workplace reps, for young teachers and for activists. Most importantly, though, this is embodied in the many coalitions and alliances which are being built at local level, whether in defence of state schools, or to promote other aspects of the vision, such as challenging child poverty, ending the school places crisis or defending every child's right to a qualified teacher[38].

The question of an alternative vision also has implications for other areas which will undoubtedly prove to be a little more challenging.

Under Britain's restrictive anti-union laws, it would be illegal for the NUT, or any union, to call a political strike. All industrial action must stem from a 'legitimate trade dispute' with the employer, narrowing the range of issues on which the union is allowed to take industrial action.

By embedding industrial action within a wider campaign, it is possible to shift the focus without compromising the legality of the action. The major debates in the media and on the streets during the strikes of 2014 were qualified teacher status, control over the curriculum and the fragmentation of the education system. Although the strikes were called over a legitimate trade dispute with the employer, the NUT managed to link this industrial dispute to issues of wider concern amongst parents and others. In this way, they mobilised public support for the strikes and used it to build a base in local communities.

However, this approach needs to be developed more thoroughly, along the lines of the Chicago Teachers' Union, from which the NUT draws much inspiration and support.[39]

More broadly, the need to directly challenge Britain's anti-trade union laws is growing ever more pressing and the question of political strikes has been on the agenda of the wider trade union movement in recent years.[40]

As one of the authors wrote in a previous article with NUT Deputy General Secretary Kevin Courtney, 'Part of our strategy to build a Stand Up for Education movement has to be to reclaim strike action as a political tool which can be used in defence of communities and of education."[41]

At some point, this course of action will necessitate making further inroads into the political sphere. What form this political intervention will take will be a crucial question for the NUT.

Conclusion

In this chapter, we have argued that, in the response of the NUT to the Global Education Reform Movement, three main characteristics have begun to emerge which set it apart from other examples – grassroots organising, community coalition building and articulating an alternative vision. We further argue that, taken together, these three characteristics constitute the emergence of an embryonic form of 'social movement unionism'. We believe that these developments are significant precisely because they have the potential to provide a real challenge to neoliberalism.

Notes

1 Sahlberg, 2010
2 Public education is usually referred to as state education in England.
3 Stevenson and Woods, 2013
4 Stevenson and Bacia, 2013
5 Weiner, date
6 Foster (2009)
7 Ball (2010)
8 Simon (date)
9 This raises interesting questions about the relationship between citizen rights and consumer rights in education, explored by Whitt (date).
10 reference
11 reference
12 Stevenson 2011
13 reference
14 For example, the announcement of the 30th June read, 'Both NUT and ATL members will take strike action on 30th June. Lecturers union UCU and civil servants in the PCS will also take action on pensions that day."
15 Greenshields 2012
16 NUT 2012 Press Release - https://www.teachers.org.uk/node/15834
17 NUT Action Sort of Strike Action Guidance - https://www.teachers.org.uk/files/instructions-for-action-short-of-strike-action.pdf
18 Personal correspondence from Alex Kenny 22/06/14
19 http://www.itv.com/news/anglia/story/2014-07-09/public-sector-workers-prepare-to-strike/

20 Fairbrother, 1996 and 2000
21 Fairbrother, 1996 and 2000
22 In fact, the precursors of these changes were evident far earlier, with copies of *Organising to Win* by Bronfenbrenner *et al* circulating within the union and senior officials meeting with key industrial relations academics to discuss organising as early as 2004/5.
23 https://www.morningstaronline.co.uk/a-ae8f-The-NUT-is-rising-to-the-academy-challenge#.VVACCflViko
24 Kelly, 1998
25 Kelly, 1998
26 https://www.morningstaronline.co.uk/a-ae8f-The-NUT-is-rising-to-the-academy-challenge#.VVACCflViko
27 Tattersall date
28 Ball 1990; Stevenson 2011
29 Gramsci 1971:57
30 Hoffman,1984
31 Hoffman, 1984
32 Ball, 1990:32
33 Gove 2013
34 Gove 2014
35 Kenway 1987
36 Ball 1990:33
37 Gramsci 1971
38 Another key aspect to this work is the development of the *Reclaiming Schools* website by a group of educational researchers who believe that 'there is an urgent need to reclaim schools from the corporate interests that increasingly drive education policy'. The authors call for a 'struggle to reclaim schools for a more optimistic vision of education" and draw their inspiration from the *Stand Up for Education* campaign.
39 See chapter 10 of this publication.
40 Ewing &Hendy, 2012
41 Courtney & Little 2014

Bibliography

Ball, S.J. (1990) *Politics and Policy Making in Education: Explorations in Policy Sociology*, London: Routledge.

Blower, C. (2014a) Empowering lay structures, *Morning Star*, 19th April.

Blower, C. (2014b) The NUT is rising to the academy challenge, *Morning Star*, 21st April.

Blower, C. (2014c) Putting the union at the heart of our communities, *Morning Star*, 22nd April.

Carter, B., Stevenson, H. and Passy, R. (2010) *Industrial Relations in Education: Transforming the School Workforce*, London: Routledge.

Courtney, K. and Little, G. (2014) Standing Up for Education: building a national campaign, *FORUM*, 56(2), 299-317. http://dx.doi.org/10.2304/forum.2014.56.2.299

Ewing, K. & Hendy, J. (2011) *Days of Action: The Legality of Protest Strikes Against Government Cuts*, Liverpool: Institute of Employment Rights.

Fairbrother, P. (1996) Workplace trade unionism in the state sector, in P. Ackers., C. Smith., and P. Smith (eds) *The new workplace and trade unions* London: Routledge.

Fairbrother, P. (2000). British trade unions facing the future. *Capital & Class*, 24(2), 11-42.

Foster, J. (2009) *The Politics of Britain's Economic Crisis*, London: Communist Party

Gove (2013) I refuse to surrender to the Marxist teachers hell-bent on destroying our schools, *Daily Mail*, 23rd March.

Gove (2014) *The Purpose of Our School Reforms*. London: DfE.

Gramsci, A. (1971) *Selections from the Prison Notebooks*, London: Lawrence & Wishart.

Greenshields, B. (2012) *Broadening the Battle Lines: The Pensions Struggle - a fight for public services and trade union organisation*, London: Communist Party.

HM Treasury (2011) Statement by the Chief Secretary to the Treasury, Rt Hon Danny Alexander MP, on Public Service Pensions. London: HM Treasury

Hoffman, J. (1984) *The Gramscian Challenge: Coercion and Consent in Marxist Political Theory*, London: Basil Blackwell.

Kelly, J. (1998) *Rethinking Industrial Relations: Mobilisation, Collectivisation and Long Waves*, London: Routledge.

Kenway, J. (1987) Left Right out: Australian Education and the Politics of Signification, *Journal of Education Policy*, 2(3), 189-204.

Sahlberg, P. (2010) *Finnish Lessons: What Can the World Learn from Educational Change in Finland?* New York: Teachers' College Press.

Simon, B. (1987) Lessons in Elitism, *Marxism Today*, September 12-17.

Simon, B (1988) *Bending the Rules: The Baker 'Reform' of Education* London: Lawrence &Wishart.

Simon, B (1991) *Education and the Social Order: British Education Since 1944 (Studies in the History of Education)*, London: Lawrence & Wishart.

Stevenson, H. (2011) Coalition education policy: Thatcherism's long shadow in *Forum: for promoting 3-19 comprehensive education*. 53 (2) 179-194.

Stevenson, H. and Bascia, N. (2013) *Teacher unions and multi-unionism: identifying issues of gender and militancy in Ontario and England*, paper presented at AERA annual meeting, San Francisco CA, 27 April-1st May.

Stevenson, H. and Wood, P. (2013) Markets, managerialism and teachers' work: the invisible hand of high stakes testing in England, International Education Journal: Comparative Perspectives 12 (2) available online at http://openjournals.library.usyd.edu.au/index.php/IEJ/article/view/7455

Tattersall, A. (2013) Power in coalition: strategies for strong unions and social change, Ithaca, NY: ILR Press.

Weiner, L. (2012) *The Future of our schools: teachers unions and social justice*, Chicago: Haymarket Books.

White, A. (2013) *Guide to Online Campaigning for Unions*, Self-Published.

10 A city transformed: lessons from the struggle of Chicago teachers

Carol Caref

THIS PAPER will focus on the issue of school closings and the related proliferation of charter schools. This issue, as much as any other, has defined the reshaping of public education in Chicago. By closing 118 schools in predominately African American neighborhoods, CPS has destabilized those neighborhoods, laid off thousands of Black teachers, and forced students to travel long distances or attend charter schools. The issue is one that the Chicago Teachers Union has invested much energy into opposing using organizing, research, communications, and political means. At this point the battle is still being fought, but there are small cracks in the ability of CPS to continue this strategy. The union, together with parents, students, and community partners, continues to push on this and other important issues.

National Context

In the U.S., 90% of students attend public schools, although in Chicago, the percentage is lower: 85%. Education is locally-run, although there are changes afoot. National standards are being introduced under the guise of 'Common Core State Standards". These common standards have been agreed to by 46 of the 50 states. They move the former education markets, composed of 50 states with different requirements, into one national market, thereby profiting the publishing companies who created the standards.

Funding differs by locality, but Illinois schools are funded mostly by property taxes; this creates great inequities, as wealthier areas have more money for schools. The state provides less than 1/3 of the education dollars in Illinois, with the rest being generated locally. Federal money accounts for only 12% of education funding, and provides token support for special education and low-income students and for free lunch programs. Federal money is distributed inequitably to states winning Race to the Top grants. The idea that education funding is a race, not a right, is one of the many issues facing the U.S. education community.

There are two teachers unions nationally: The American Federation of Teachers (AFT), to which the Chicago Teachers Union (CTU) belongs, and the National Education Association (NEA). The organizations have different histories and structures; AFT is more common in the cities and NEA more common in suburbs and rural areas. There have been attempts to merge the two unions, but that has not happened on a national scale. The two organizations in New York and California are merged unions. Just about half of all teachers are union members, 24 states have "right to work" laws which make it difficult for unions to organize.

Most AFT and NEA locals have the right to bargain collectively. In Chicago, the collective bargaining has, until recently, followed a traditional structure. Union leaders met in secret with bargaining team members from Chicago Public Schools. Although members knew in general what CTU was demanding at the bargaining table, the details were unknown. In the negotiations leading to the 2012-2015 contract, CTU created an open bargaining process. The negotiating team was expanded to include 30 CTU leaders, in addition to the usual officers, attorneys, and staff members. These 30 leaders played an important role, as they explained to the CPS team the importance of each contract item under discussion. During "caucus" breaks in negotiations, the expanded team discussed what response CTU should give to various CPS offers. Communications to the membership kept them abreast of bargaining developments. As 2015 approaches, there is talk of expanding this open process even more widely, to include students, parents, and interested community members, as was done recently in St. Paul, Minnesota negotiations.

Throughout the United States, local school boards make decisions about the education of students in the locality. In most cases, these school boards are elected. In Chicago, the school board is appointed by the mayor. Chicago's unelected school board consistently makes decisions that are in line with the mayor's financial plans, but at odds with the city's actual education needs. The expansion of charter schools is one example of this. Charter schools are publicly funded, but privately managed. Even the charters that call themselves non-profit have made money from real estate deals, from huge administrative salaries, or from outlandish payments to the "parent" organization of the charter management company. In this endeavor, they have been successful, but in educating students, they have proven no more successful than publicly-funded, publicly-run CPS schools.

The Neo-Liberal Assault

In 1995, the Illinois state legislature instituted mayoral control over Chicago's public schools. Signaling the corporate community's intrusion into education, Chicago Public Schools (CPS) would now have a "CEO" with business experience instead of a Superintendent with education experience. A few years later, the Civic Committee of the Commercial Club of Chicago issued recommendations that became the foundation of CPS' Renaissance 2010 policy. Subsequently, educational policies took on the character of business practices. Practices like competition, investment in "winners" versus disinvestment in "losers" and outcomes-based planning all replaced proven educational practices of collaboration, more attention to those in greater need, rich curricula, and emphasis on hard-to-measure qualities such as creativity, critical thinking, and love of learning. It is hard to believe that the corporate community's interest in education is unrelated to the profit motive. The U.S. education market is a $500 billion business! While the details of how corporations make profits from this industry are still unfolding, the details of the harm to students from business-based policies are apparent.

The closing of schools to turn the education of Chicago's students over to charter management organizations is a failed policy. While charters began as a vision for teacher-led, unionized schools that would lead to innovations to be shared across all schools, charter operators have pursued a different agenda. As a result, charter schools perform no better, and in many instances worse, than comparable neighborhood schools. The slash-and-burn approach to schooling that lies at the heart of the "charter bargain" must be abandoned and replaced with policies based on proven supports for schools in need. By continuing to accelerate school closings, "turnarounds" and charter school proliferation, CPS ignores the evidence that their policy is a failure. The Districts' actions are destructive, particularly in low-income, African-American communities.

School actions and charter proliferation are concentrated in the African-American South and West Sides of the city. These areas have lowest median family incomes and frequently include demolished public housing sites. More than 95 percent of turnaround schools are located in census tracts[1] with the lowest median family income range. There are few school actions or schools run by charter management operators in areas of the city where the wealthiest Chicagoans live. The policies of CPS only further the destabilization of neighborhoods already disrupted by housing and employment crises, poverty, and racial segregation.

Although some exceptions do exist, in general, the 20-year-old policy of moving children from school to school has failed dramatically. On average, educational outcomes for CPS students have not improved, despite claims to the contrary. Instead, the policy of closing, turning around, consolidating or phasing out neighborhood schools and turning the education of Chicago's students over to charter management companies has:

● increased racial segregation in schools in general
● depleted stable African-American neighborhood schools in particular
● increased student mobility, particularly in areas with high concentrations of school actions
● promoted disrespect and poor treatment of teachers by blaming them instead of CPS policy for under-performing schools
● expanded unnecessary testing while decreasing opportunities for deep, conceptual learning
● increased punitive student discipline

The "underutilization crisis" of 2013 was manufactured largely to justify the replacement of neighborhood schools by privatized charters. CPS claimed that it needed to "right-size" the number of schools to match the number of students, but that position is not supported by the facts. Actually, CPS has opened more than 100 new schools and acquired or constructed space to educate close to 50,000 additional students in the last ten years. Many of the new schools were placed in areas where existing schools had been closed. As part of the Gates Compact, CPS has pledged to open at least 60 new schools run by charter management organizations. If the problem is "underutilization" or "under enrollment," why spend hundreds of millions to create new schools?

While the policy of school closing and opening has not moved education in Chicago forward in any significant way, the benefits to charter school operators, private testing companies, real estate interests, and wealthy bankers are growing.

The Chicago Board of Education's facilities decisions have a long and controversial political history, but the most recent iteration can be traced to 1995, when the Illinois state legislature granted complete control of the schools to the Mayor of Chicago. The city was once 'hailed as a pioneer for putting local school decision-making into the hands of elected school councils,"[2] yet the practical operational effect of mayoral control was a concentration of power in the mayor's office and CPS central office. This shift made education policy less democratic and increasingly directed by business community and politicians, with reduced input by actual educators. Since mayoral control began in 1995, the District saw increases, positives (graduation) and negatives (racial achievement gaps and percent of students leaving the system). Huge resource disparities proliferated selective enrollment schools, turnarounds and charters received state of the art facilities, equipment and supplies, while neighborhood schools serving low-income students of color deteriorated. These disparities, supposedly established to give "choice" to parents, reflect a two-tiered system akin to what is commonly understood to be apartheid.

Disparities grew under Arne Duncan, who was tapped to lead CPS in 2001. During Duncan's tenure, the number of facilities decisions and school actions skyrocketed. In 2004, CPS launched the Renaissance 2010 initiative (Ren10), with the intention of improving schools by closing at least 60 low-performing neighborhood schools and opening 100 new schools in their place mostly a mix of charter, contract, and performance schools, but also several magnet, selective enrollment, and new neighborhood schools. Ren10 was based on recommendations from the Civic Committee of the Commercial Club of Chicago [3] and the federal guidelines of No Child Left Behind, which allowed Districts to close or turn around schools that failed to make Adequate Yearly Progress (AYP) on state exams.

Throughout the Ren10 process, CPS had *no* master facilities plan. Without any coherent strategy, CPS phased out, consolidated, and turned around 17 schools in early 2012, in addition to the dozens of schools acted against in the previous 10 years. Facilities decisions were so ad hoc and haphazard that pressure from parents, teachers and community groups for a moratorium on school actions gained traction in the Illinois state capitol in 2009 and 2010. A bill that would have put the brakes on this policy was watered down during the legislative process (CPS lobbied heavily in opposition to the bill), and the resulting legislation did not call for a moratorium. Instead, the state created the Chicago Educational Facilities Task Force (CEFTF) to oversee CPS' facilities decisions. Under the law, CPS is required to create a 10-year master facilities plan, but the District missed the January, 2013, deadline and the plan finally released in September, 2013, was severely deficient.

It is unsurprising that the 'reform' plan of the corporate community, represented by the Commercial Club, focused on gutting neighborhood schools and punishing teachers for the sake of private profits. Chicago's corporate leadership has been attempting to control public schools and weaken public sector unions for more than 100 years.[4] Furthermore, since mayoral control began in 1995 and gentrification has spread across the city in earnest, Chicago's political and corporate elite have used school reform as a strategy to attract and retain middle class families in the city, while controlling and closing schools in low-income communities of color. [5]

In all, tens of thousands of students have been directly impacted by CPS School Actions since 2001. [6] 88 percent of students affected are African-American. Schools that are over 99 percent students of color ("Apartheid schools"[7]) have been the primary target of CPS school actions representing over 80 percent of all affected schools. Black communities have been hit the hardest—three out of every four affected schools were economically poor and intensely segregated African-American schools. [8]

These students face a wide range of challenges outside of school, including high levels of violence and trauma, but are still expected to serve as test subjects for unproven school reform schemes. Schools serving wealthier and whiter students would never be expected to fire the entire school staff; yet, this disruptive tactic has been used repeatedly on the predominantly Black South and West sides of Chicago. Moreover, school actions like closures and turnarounds disproportionately target experienced African-American teachers. In 2011, African-Americans 26 percent of all teachers—represented 65 percent of teachers in schools tapped for closure and 40 percent of tenured teachers laid off. [9] The number of African-American teachers will likely decline even more, as Black teachers make up only 20 percent of the District's teachers with five or fewer years of experience. [10] The proliferation of charter schools also contributes to the decline of Black educators and the racial imbalance between the teachers and the students in CPS, Only 22 percent of teachers identified as Black among CPS charter schools in 2011, compared to the roughly 60 percent of Black students in charters.

The massive school closings that have been part of CPS' broader strategy dating back to the 1990s have drastic consequences: They tear apart school communities; disrupt deep and strong relationships between students, parents, and teachers; and dismantle organizations that are often the only center of stability and safety for students. Overall, students have not benefited from schools closings or turnarounds. Despite the illusion of "choice," students affected by school actions have most often landed in schools that struggle as much as their previous school. [11] In a consolidation or closure, those students are sent to a receiving school that may be several miles from their original neighborhood school. The transferred students have to navigate transportation challenges and cross gang territories that put them at risk of violence. Additionally, studies have shown that student achievement in the receiving schools is negatively affected by the school closings. [12]

Charter and turnaround schools do not serve all neighborhood students. If the original school endured a closure and restarted as a charter, students in the new school usually have a different composition than the previous mix of students fewer special education students, fewer students from the neighborhood and fewer low-income students. [13] Charter schools require an application process for lottery admissions, which has the effect of weeding out students who have difficult family situations or less interest in school. *The school action policies of CPS have a disproportionately negative impact on the students who most need policies that actually improve the quality of their education.*

While school closings and disruptions have required vast resources at both the District and school level, simple yet effective interventions to help students have been defunded and ignored over for decades. The *Chicago Tribune's* recent series on truancy at the elementary level in CPS sheds light on the tragic and complex life struggles that impede the ability of so many children living in poverty to make it to school.[14] As with other challenges associated with the effects of poverty and segregation in Chicago, truancy is especially prevalent in South and West Side communities. As many as 20 percent of Black elementary school students missed more than four weeks of school in 2011 due to truancy, gaps in enrollment and absences.

The reasons for truancy have their roots in poverty and the difficult familial circumstances of the students, but schools can still help children when they have the resources to individually and personally monitor the students who consistently fail to appear in school. The *Tribune* series indicates that for some suburban school districts coping with rising poverty, the use of truant officers and social workers to reach out to students and their families are of crucial importance in making sure children don't end up out of school and forgotten.[15] Truant officers are long gone from CPS the last one was fired in 1992. Like other essential support staff, even when CPS had them, there were never enough truant officers to go around, with most working in at least three schools.[16] The data from that period indicate that truancies went up in the years following the loss of truant officers.

Instead of providing schools with resources and funding so that they can properly offer wrap-around supports, the District has attacked and shut down schools they label 'failing."Schools that have been closed, turned around and phased out all had histories of high chronic truancy in the years leading up to the disruptive school actions. High schools that faced school actions from 2008 to 2011 had chronic truancy rates averaging over 50 percent in the years prior to closure. Elementary schools that faced school actions over those years had nearly one in five students chronically truant. The District's contradictory response to such evident need for targeted support shows how misguided the policies of austerity and school closures are.

The Union Response

In June of 2010, a slate of teachers, the Caucus of Rank-and-File Educators [CORE] won leadership of the 30,000-member CTU. Members voted for the CORE slate because the caucus had focused on organizing against the neo-liberal assault, while their predecessors ignored it. CORE fought against the closing or 'turn around" of 25 schools that had been placed on the 2009 'Hit List."They attended and organized at every hearing, held protests downtown and in neighborhoods, wrote letters to the editor, and united with community and parent groups to fight the school actions. They organized 500 people to attend a meeting during a January blizzard to plan the fight. In the end, nine schools were removed from the list not enough, but more than previously, when CPS had carte blanche to close and turn around at will.

In 2010, the list of 15 school slated for action ended up being eight, after more protests organized by CORE and their community partners in the Grass Roots Education Movement (GEM). Most of the eight schools were turned around. This process leads to the dismissal of every adult in the building (including lunchroom workers, custodians, and other support workers, as well as teachers and principals). Workers may "reapply" for their jobs, but are seldom rehired. Turnaround is mainly a ploy to turn over schools to private operators, such as Academy for Urban School Leadership (AUSL), although unlike charters, the schools are still subject to CPS policies.

In addition to leading the fight against school closings and turnarounds, CORE built its internal strength. They held a study group on Naomi Klein's The Shock Doctrine. They met often, recruited members, and raised money. They hammered out their principles, and agreed to these:

- Member Driven Union – The focus of the caucus is to respond to and represent the voice of the members.
- Transparency & Accountability – All actions, elections and finances shall be open to all members for inspection and as such are open to public debate and discussion within the membership.
- Education for All – CORE fights for equitable high quality education for all students and seeks to establish and maintain partnerships among parents, students, community, and labor organizations for this purpose.
- Defense of Publicly Funded Public Education – Whereas public education is under attack from a well-funded group of business interests, politicians, privatizers and enemies of publicly funded public education, CORE seeks to defend publicly funded public education as the last bastion of democratic expression and hope for students in all public schools across Chicago.
- Strong Contract – A strong Agreement between the Chicago Teacher's Union and the Board of Education shall ensure that working conditions and compensation provide for optimal teaching and learning.

The principles and actions proved to be in line with what CTU members wanted to see in their leaders, and those elected from the CORE slate have continued to lead the union with those principles in mind.

The change in direction led to a noticeable improvement in teacher morale. The new CTU leadership made several changes to the focus of the union. They allocated the resources needed to create a CTU organizing department, and a research department, neither of which had previously existed. They beefed up the communications department, and members began to regularly see quotations from CTU leaders in the newspaper as well as radio and television interviews. The legislative department was reinvigorated as well. The new leaders aligned the salaries of union staffers with teachers' pay. In addition, they created a summer program that trained activist teachers to organize their peers and formed contract committees in every school. They increased trainings for the elected union leaders in each school, known as delegates.

In September of 2012, the CTU published *The Schools Chicago's Students Deserve*. The report made the case for immediate district-wide enforcement of practical and proven solutions to improve the academic performance of Chicago's students. It presented the argument that the education children receive should not depend on zip code, family income, or racial background, although statistics show that all too often those are the deciding factors. It was the answer to the neo-liberal narrative about the "reforms" necessary to fix education. This paper became the cornerstone of CTU's advocacy.

The Schools Chicago's Students Deserve also took on the funding issue. It attacked schemes such as Tax Increment Financing (TIFs), which diverted money from schools and other public projects into the pockets of bankers and developers. It called for fair school funding, progressive taxation, and an end to corporate subsidies and loopholes. The paper itemized the educational improvements that could be tied to these funding increases.

CTU turned every attack into an organizing opportunity. In last 2010, the billionaire-backed Stand for Children (aka 'Stand on Children') donated hundreds of thousands of dollars to Illinois politicians for their election campaigns. Those politicians then held "education hearings" to push Stand's agenda. CTU organized hundreds of members to attend the hearings, published research to dispute Stand's claims, and lobbied legislators against the "reform" agenda. The result was legislation that was not great, but far less harmful than it would have been without CTU's efforts.

In 2011, CPS started demanding "waiver votes" (a contract clause allowed members to waive a section of the contract for their school, with a majority vote), to allow for a longer school day. CTU had meetings in virtually every school scheduled to take a waiver vote, which resulted in a "no" vote in all but a handful of schools. The effort led to the election of delegates in dozens of schools without them, energized members used to having no recourse against CPS demands, and created a basis for further organizing efforts.

The Stand on Children law passed in 2011 included several provisions designed to make it harder for CTU to strike. The union was able to turn every one of those provisions around and use it to its advantage. The law required a yes vote of 75% of the membership (not just the voters) in order to strike. The CTU held delegate trainings, mock votes, and practice votes in the schools, so that when the actual vote came, the organizational apparatus was in shape to guarantee that every member voted. The draconian measures implemented by Chicago Public Schools, including the denial of a negotiated 4% raise, together with the confidence the CTU leadership had instilled in members, meant that most members were ready to vote "yes" to a strike. When the actual vote came, 90% of members and 98% of those voting said "yes" to authorization of a strike.

The law also required that an impartial "fact finder" look at disputed issues. The fact finder looked at the CPS numbers and the CTU numbers and agreed that the CTU numbers were right. He recommended:

- A 12.6 percent raise to account for his finding that teachers would be working a 19.6 percent longer day and year.
- An additional 2.25 percent cost-of-living raise.
- Step and lane increases. The district wants to scrap these raises based on seniority and education in favor of a merit pay program, which the union opposes.

It was obvious that this favorable decision did not happen in a vacuum, but was the result of the hard work of the organizing, research, and communications department. The large turnout of CTU members to vote, rally, and march in the streets; the evidence compiled by research; and the publicity generated by communications, all played a role in this decision.

A May 23, 2012, rally had galvanized members and the public alike. The spirited gathering of 4000 (all that could fit in the hall) joined another 2000 CTU members and supporters for a march around downtown Chicago that took over the streets and foreshadowed the daily downtown rallies that would later occur during the strike.

By September 2012, the city had still refused to offer CTU members a decent contract. The House of Delegates voted unanimously to go on strike. It was the first teacher strike in Chicago in 25 years. A *Truthout* review of Micah Uetricht's book *Strike for America: Chicago Teachers Against Austerity* sums up the strike this way:

> "The entire city felt transformed", Uetricht writes. "Teachers were engaged in highly visible, militant, mass action, and there was a widespread sense throughout the city of the legitimacy and necessity of such action – for educators and for other workers ... The union held mass rallies nearly every day with tens of thousands of teachers and their supporters ... Teachers began organizing actions themselves, independent of the CTU leadership. No union staffers planned the small marches on the mayor's house during the strike; teachers planned these themselves."

This had an enormous impact on union activists because the ability to do what they felt was necessary – without having to jump through bureaucratic approval hoops – gave the members a sense of CTU ownership. Eight days later, when a tentative contract settlement was reached, they voted to extend the strike by two days to give themselves a chance to thoroughly digest the document rather than allow Lewis and the negotiating team to tell them what it said. 'For the first time," Uetricht writes, 'teachers were studying every word of their contract, the principal document governing their work lives." On October 3, 79 percent of the membership voted in favor of the accord.

And the lessons? *Strike for America* concludes that 'Rather than trying to meet free-market education reformers in the middle on their proposals to privatize schools or increase teacher evaluations based on standardized testing – as national teachers unions have done – the CTU was uncompromising in its rejection of the demands of Mayor Rahm Emmanuel and corporate reform groups. Rather than allowing such groups to paint the union as a roadblock to educational progress, the CTU put forth its own positive proposals to reform schools, grounded in an unapologetic vision of progressive education that would be funded by taxing the rich."

Footnotes

1   Census tracts are small areas within counties that are used by the U.S. Census Bureau to track and analyze socio-economic and population data over time and across geographies. Since they are small (between 1,500 and 8,000 residents), they are thought to be relatively homogenous in terms of the characteristic information n the census collects about the people that live there. For more information about census tracts, visit the U.S. Census Bureau website: www.census.gov

2 Lipman, P., Smith, J., Guststein, E., & Dallacqua, L. (February 2012). Examining CPS' plan to close, turn-around, or phase out 17 schools. *Data and Democracy Project: Investing in Neighborhoods*, Research Paper Series, Paper #3. Retrieved from http://www.uic.edu/educ/ceje/resources.html

3 Civic Committee of the Commercial Club of Chicago (2003). *Left behind: A report of the education committee*.Chicago, IL. Note: the Civic Committee members are Chicago's corporate elite, the chairmen and CEO's of the top corporations operating in Chicago. For a list of its members and initiatives, visit http://civiccommittee.org/index.html.

4 Shipps, D. (2006). School Reform, Corporate Style: Chicago 1880-2000. Lawrence, KS: University of Kansas Press.

5 Lipman, P. (2009). Making sense of Renaissance 2010 school policy in Chicago: Race, class, and the cultural politics of neoliberal urban restructuring. (Working Paper GCP-09-02). Retrieved from Great Cities Institute Working Paper: http://www.uic.edu/cuppa/gci/publications/workingpaperseries/pdfs/GCP-09-02_Lipman.pdf

6 School actions include Closings, Turnarounds, Consolidations, and Phase-outs.

7 Apt term referring to schools with 99 percent or more non-white students, coined by Gary Orfield, Co-Director of The Civil Rights Project of UCLA

8 Referring to schools that were at least 90 percent Black and at least 75 percent Free or Reduced lunch.

9 Data from 2011 ISBE Teacher Service Records and CPS Position Rosters.

10 Caref, C., & Jankov, P. (2012, Feb 16). The schools Chicago's students deserve. Retrieved from http://www.ctunet.com/blog/text/SCSD_Report-02-16-2012-1.pdf

11 de la Torre, M., & Gwynne, J. (2009). *When schools close: Effects on displaced students in Chicago Public Schools*. Chicago: Consortium on Chicago School Research.

12 Brummet, Quentin (2012). The effect of school closings on student achievement. Retrieved from https://www.msu.edu/~brummetq/SC_Students.pdf

13 de la Torre, M., Allensworth, E., Jagesic, S., Sebastian, J., & Salmonowicz, M. (2012). *Turning Around Low-Performing Schools in Chicago*. Chicago: Consortium on Chicago School Research http://ccsr.uchicago.edu/content/publications.php?pub_id=163

14 Jackson, D., Marx, G., Richards, A. (2012, Nov. 11). An empty-desk epidemic. *Chicago Tribune*. Retrieved from http://articles.chicagotribune.com/2012-11-11/news/ct-met-truancy-mainbar-20121111_1_west-side-school-elementary-grades-school-for-four-weeks

15 Marx, G., Jackson, D. (2012, Nov. 12). Small town succeeds where Chicago fails. *Chicago Tribune*. Retrieved from http://articles.chicagotribune.com/2012-11-12/news/ct-met-truancy-galesburg-20121112_1_truancy-hearings-school-attendance-outreach-workers

16 Forte, L.W. (1994). As truancy rises, agencies launch new tactics. *Catalyst Chicago*. Vol V. No 8. Retrieved from http://www.catalyst-chicago.org/assets/assets/extra/1994/4CATMay1994.pdf

11 Reimagining and remaking education: remarks to the NUT–Teacher Solidarity conference

Lois Weiner

FIRST MY thanks to the NUT and its International Committee for hosting this conference. In doing so you have provided resources, material and human, at a time when you are involved in an intense struggle to defend education, our profession, children, and teachers' dignity as workers in your own country. In sponsoring this event, the NUT models three concepts that I will put forth as essential for development of new kinds of relationships among teachers unions globally: a critical analysis of neoliberalism's international project; a re-definition of solidarity; and acommitment to move beyond resistance to creation of alternatives. In my remarks today I discuss what these three concepts mean for research, researchers, and activists who share a commitment to reversing the neoliberal project.

The role of academics in defending public education and teachers unions is extraordinarily important today. Both higher and lower education are being transformed by policies that aim to make all human activity, including intellectual and artistic work, subject to what is called the discipline of the market, but is, in fact, the control of powerful elites who manage capitalism and increasingly use the state without political challenge. [1] A divide exists between academics doing critical work in education and teachers unions, a topic I explore elsewhere. But in sponsoring this conference and the Research Collaborative on the teachersolidarity.com website, the NUT has made a significant contribution to bringing together two groups who need to collaborate.

In research conferences, we assume participants will turn off their phones. However, I ask that we turn ON our phones but turn OFF the ringers. Please use social media to publicize the ideas we discuss. These ideas differ very sharply from what we hear and see in mass media. We need to use social media to create a counter narrative. My twitter handle is @drloisweiner. I hope someone will come up with a hashtag?

Steven Klees has observed that the architects of the neoliberal project take positions that 'have no relation to evidence. Theirs is a remorseless logic in the service of an ideology." But Klees argues rather than limiting our response to empirical data that contradicts their findings, 'We must lay to rest the logic of such proof and move on to public policy debates that incorporate a very different logic, one that recognizes the limits of expertise and one that reflects that different views of 'evidence' can only be applied within democratic participative processes that give voice and power to those currently treated so inequitably." (p. 23) [2] Teachers unions at their best sustain those 'democratic participative processes," arguably more effectively than any other advocacy group in education, so bringing researchers together with activists as you have done today is quite important in creating a counter-narrative to the story of what's wrong with education and how to fix it.

The first task we have is to deepen and sharpen critical understanding of neoliberalism's international transformation of education. These changes are altering teachers work in ways that go well beyond the scope of traditional contract negotiations. Standardized testing, privatization of the education sector, including teacher and school evaluation, creation of private schools paid for by public money, whether called 'free schools," "academies" or "charter schools," are undermining the profession and children's education. Unions and their members need research to help them devise strategies to win public support in the struggle to turn back attacks on the profession. Academics in the US are beginning to realize that teachers unions can be an invaluable ally in social struggles against neoliberalism's educational project, mainly because of the exciting renewal of teacher unionism in Chicago. But as we have seen in the workshops today, while collaborations on a national level are needed, they are also insufficient.

We need to learn from resistance in other nations. One of the most powerful lessons about collaborations between researchers and activists is Hugo Aboites' observation that a powerful student movement in Mexico created space for researchers, who in turn contributed to the movement against the latest education reforms by touring Mexico to educate teachers and citizens to a critical view of what was in store. [3]

Practical problems need to be solved for collaborations between researchers and unions to occur. Often the knowledge we produce is abstracted from the demands of the immediate struggle and therefore not applicable without intermediary support. Often the venues in which we make our work known are not easily accessed by activists. But as we see from the Chicago Teachers Union, when a union creates a research department that has a critical lens, it can issue reports that put unions on the offensive, in part by opening the door to collaborations with researchers in universities who are critical of educational policy but may not necessarily understand the union perspective. Another creative solution is the BCTF support for www.teachersolidarity.com website's online Research Collaborative archive.

However, in embracing collaboration we should note that when researchers adopt a "scholarship of public engagement"[4] they face a tension. In activism we use knowledge to make decisions. In research our aim is to create questions, bring complexity, pose problems. While the knowledge we seek as researchers is informed by our ideals and ideology, the most useful research does not permit ideals to determine the conclusions. In this process we may reach conclusions that make us and the unions uncomfortable. For this reason, I suggest that we understand the role of a researcher who is a supporter of teachers unions as a "critical friend." Being a critical friend means posing questions and making suggestions that may disrupt the way things are understood and done, challenging assumptions and practices deeply ingrained in the union. Those most responsible for the union's functioning are often most sensitive to what is, accurately, perceived as criticism. But criticism is precisely what we as researchers must offer, along of course, with support.

So in this role of critical friend of teacher unionism, I suggest that critical analysis of our current situation must begin with recognition that neoliberalism's ideological and material victories were and are abetted by inequalities in schooling and society that teachers unions accepted, along with social democratic parties, in labor's post-WW2 pact with capital. [5] The contours of what Panitch and Gindin refer to as "corporate productivism"[6] in the private sector provided the framework for collective bargaining for public employees, including teachers unions. Labor traded many rights to challenge power relations on the "shop floor," for government protections for collective bargaining. While changes to labor law and collective bargaining legislation gave teachers unions stability and the strength to negotiate improved wages and benefits for members, the framework also locked teachers and students into arrangements of schooling that resulted in unequal educational outcomes, within nation states and internationally.

We must confront this history because the legacy undercuts our struggle. Neoliberalism wins its ideological and material victories in part because of capital's control of the state and media. But its success has been abetted by its ability to expose inequalities that we have not challenged with the same vigor we have used to pursue economic benefits for our members. To reverse this cycle we have to be self-critical and frank, acknowledging that while we did not cause inequality, unions have not done all they might to challenge social and economic inequality within nations and globally. We should now use our power to insist on a global debate about how schools and society are organized, whose interests they serve, and why. This debate requires a more critical analysis of global economic and political realities.

Nowhere is this clearer than in the presumption, to quote Arne Duncan, that education is "the one true path out of poverty."[7] This perspective obviates the state's obligation to address poverty through economic policy, for example outlawing poverty-level wages and creating well-paying jobs that support a sustainable economy. Structural unemployment and the race to the bottom in wages and working conditions sentence the vast majority of the world's people to a lifetime of economic insecurity and desperation. International testing is designed to obscure this reality, to persuade parents and citizens that "there is no alternative" to a global economy that consists of workers of every nation competing against one another for work that can be easily shifted to a nation that will hyper-exploit its own people, providing huge profits for multinational corporations and wealth for a small sliver of the population. Schooling is not and cannot be the "one true path out of poverty" for the vast majority of the world's children because the global capitalist economy, supported by military intervention when needed, consigns millions to unemployment and work that pays poverty wages.

At the same time, we need to say that schooling and teaching do count, that teachers' work when supported as it should, can improve children's lives. Schools are "places where social reproduction occurs but also where human agency matters and makes a difference in students' lives." (p. 49) [8] Neoliberal reforms resonate with many parents precisely because they want the same opportunity for their children to compete for good jobs that children of affluent parents have. Calls for schooling that makes children happy and develops creativity will not by themselves assuage parents' fears that their children will not be strong competitors in an increasingly punishing labor market.

Unless we educate parents to the real facts of economic life, our opponents will continue to exploit successfully the utterly hypocritical and inaccurate claim that it is they who protect the poor and oppressed against us, we who have more and therefore are said to want to maintain the status quo to advantage our children.

While it does some important work, the Education International, whose policies are strongly aligned with the desires of its two most powerful member organizations, the American Federation of Teachers and the National Education Association, has been unwilling to shift to an oppositional role. [9] Instead the EI bases its involvement with international agencies, the World Bank in particular, on an assumption it should persuade world leaders to return to the post-war compact. One insurmountable problem with this strategy is that capitalism rejects the compact. The powerful, super-wealthy elites who control governments and media want to destroy unions' power as well as the gains they have made for working people.

But even if we could win back the arrangement that was struck in creating collective bargaining legislation, it was a Faustian deal. Labor was bureaucratized and weakened by the quid pro quo that took away its right to intervene directly on issues that go to the heart of work, challenge power relations in the workplace. [10] We see this problem in collective bargaining for teachers as we now try to push back on changes to teachers' work, our professional autonomy and judgment about how and what we teach, over which we cannot negotiate. This is not a past to which we should try to return, even if we could.

A new generation of teachers is being politicized and radicalized very rapidly. Just as we see a global footprint of neoliberalism's global project in education (with important national differences), so we can now detect a footprint of resistance. One reason international work is so vital is that it enables us to borrow and adapt ideas, just as our opponents do. We need not and should not wait for successful strategies to emerge spontaneously in our own communities or countries. One element in the emerging footprint is new kinds of alliances with parents and community, taking traditional coalition work to a different terrain. This is territory that can make unions uncomfortable because they must share power in ways that are often unfamiliar and difficult to manage with legal strictures of collective bargaining.

These new types of alliances are supporting teacher activists where they feel too isolated and weak to speak and act as union members. Teachers are forming organizations with parents and students based on clearly articulated, shared principles that include social justice issues as well as concerns that teachers unions traditionally address. For example, Colorado teachers and parents who initially came together to 'Opt-Out'(of testing) have developed a state-wide caucus that includes both AFT and NEA members, as well as groups organizing students opposed to testing. North Carolina teachers have developed a state-wide reform group in their NEA affiliate and are working with Moral Mondays, a civil rights campaign organized by churches and supported by the few labor unions in North Carolina.

These alliances, in turn, generate new tactics and strategies. Here again, I think we can learn from what has occurred in Mexico, described in the paper by Hugo Aboites.

So, coupled with the demonstrations and marches teachers in several states organized "congresses" as they were called, which reunited hundreds of parents, in one occasion; large numbers of students in another; also communities and parents. From all this, new proposals for education started to emerge. This led to a re-appreciation of many projects organized by teachers and communities founded years before. In one of these projects, pre-hispanic languages were rescued as well as the culture they belonged to..Teachers and communities also organized projects of production and services to benefit students and the whole community. In some states, full-fledged alternative schools were created, and all the schools of the state rejected standardized testing.

We have until now been on the defensive. To shift to the offensive requires putting forward a new narrative of what we want from and in schools and new kinds of activism, moving beyond contract unionism and the strategies associated with it, including the strike. Though the strike has long been and can still be a powerful weapon, it too is limited in its effect when the employer is willing to weather the loss – which is now the case in much of the world. Alternative tactics are emerging: parents occupying schools to resist school closings in Chicago and Newark; teachers boycotting standardized tests in individual schools, school systems, and countries. In Mexico we see resistance shifting to the offense: teachers occupying schools with parents, making schools sites of human emancipation; teachers, together with one another, joined by parents and community, taking back their schools from the powerful elites who aim to eliminate democratic control of education are succeeding in doing so. What has occurred in Mexico suggests an additional strategy to the "rolling strikes" that have been adopted. Why not have "rolling occupations"? Instead of walking out, invite parents and community to join the school staff to make the school liberated territory, for a day emancipating teachers and students from the drudgery and control of a curriculum powerful elites dictate is necessary to make them compete for jobs.

Very often international work is the provenance of a small sector of union activists or officials. While this is understandable, it is also dangerous because commitments to international work are often seen by members as siphoning off resources better spent at home. One role for researchers is to help unions and teachers explore the impacts of international policy on their own work. In the end space for meaningful international work depends on the union developing a presence in the school site, having members who understand that *they* are the union [11] and that "union issues" for teachers must address power struggles about who decides what we teach and how. The context of struggle over one's own work, with work being broadly defined beyond contract and economic concerns, supports' members' understanding the need to receive – and provide – solidarity, starting in their own school, extending to their nations and globally.

Reimagining and remaking education, development of a vision constituent members of unions share, is essential for forging authentic relations of solidarity among unions globally. It is this vision rather than a particular set of organizational relations that should define our work. All who support the vision and principles deserve support. A redefined solidarity means that we in London send a message of support to the British Columbia Teachers Federation (BCTF), which takes on strike action this week. We call on the EI to do the same. Is the BCTF a member of the EI? No. Does this matter? No. BCTF members are defending teachers' rights to give all children the education they deserve by having a workable class size and composition. Their struggle is the same teachers throughout the world have to wage and institutional memberships and national borders ought not influence relations of solidarity.[12]

Another way we might operationalize the principles I have described would be to draft a statement on control of curriculum and standardized testing, pointing out how international testing, PISA in particular, degrades education and is based on the faulty assumption that globally workers have to compete for jobs in a race to the bottom, in a process that often destroys the environment. We might circulate this statement for support among researchers, unions and advocacy organizations. Affiliates of the EI might then present it as a motion, directing the EI to end its collaboration on testing and involvement with the international agencies (and corporations) that design and administer the tests.

The agenda I have outlined is admittedly ambitious but so are the aims of our opponents. They aim to destroy our profession because we educate the next generation. We are a threat to their control over social, political, and economic relations. We cannot win by following the old rules or looking backward to what has been lost. Key to our success is international work among unions, defined as our mutual and collective reimagining and remaking of education to develop the full potential of all children.

Footnotes

1 *The Global Assault on Teaching, Teachers, and Their Unions: Stories for Resistance*, edited by Mary Compton and Lois Weiner (New York: Palgrave Macmillan, 2008).

2 Steven J. Klees, 'Privatization and Neo-Liberalism: Ideology and Evidence in Rhetorical Reforms,''. *Current Issues in Comparative Education* 1, no. 2 Spring (1999) 2002: 19-26, Teachers College, Columbia University, 13 May 2013 <http://devweb.tc.columbia.edu/i/a/document/25645_1_2_Klees.pdf>.

3 Hugo Aboites, 'The Unexpected Crop: Social Insurgency and New Alternatives for Education in Mexico,"paper presented at the Global Education 'Reform'': Building Resistance and Solidarity (London England: National Union of Teachers, International Solidarity Committee, 24 May 2014).

4 Michael J. Dumas and Gary Anderson, 'Qualitative Research as Policy Knowledge: Framing Policy Problems and Transforming Education from the Ground up,''. *Education Policy Analysis Archives* 22, no. 11 17 February 2014: 1-21, Arizona State University http://epaa.asu.edu/ojs/article/view/1483/1201.

5 Nelson Lichtenstein, *A Contest of Ideas. Capital, Politics, and Labor* (Urbana: Univeristy of Illinois Press, 2013).

6 Leo Panitch and Sam Gindin, *The Making of Global Capitalism. The Political Economy of American Empire* (New York: Verso, 2012).

7 *U.S. Department of Education Awards Promise Neighborhoods Planning Grants*. Press Release, 21 September 2010, U.S. Department of Education, 15 March 2013 http://www.ed.gov/news/press-releases/us-department-education-awards-promise-neighborhoods-planning-grants.

8   Amy Stuart Wells et al., *Review of Research in Education*, edited by Robert E. Floden (Washington, D.C.: American Educational Research Association, 2004), 47-99.

9   Lois Weiner, *The Future of Our Schools. Teachers Unions and Social Justice* (Chicago: Haymarket Books, 2012).

10 Nelson Lichtenstein, *A Contest of Ideas. Capital, Politics, and Labor* (Urbana: Univeristy of Illinois Press, 2013).

11 Stephanie Ross, "Varieties of Social Unionism: Towards a Framework for Comparison,"*Just Labour: A Canadian Journal of Work and Society* 11, no. 16-34 (Autumn 2007).

12 Note: Subsequent to the paper being delivered, conference members subsequently voted a message of support to the BCTF and the EI issued a statement.

Note from editor Since the May 2014 conference, Education International has launched a major campaign against privatisation, targeting the global edubusinesses, such as Pearson, who are engaged in testing and in the provision of 'low-cost' for-profit provision in the Global South.

Afterword: We are the Penicillin to the GERM!

Kristine Mayle

GOOD EVENING. First I'd like to share greetings from our president, Karen Lewis. She is sorry she couldn't make it but is still in recovery. She and I thank you for all the well-wishes she's received from the NUT. I am excited to be back speaking with my sisters and brothers of the NUT. I've watched in excitement your various work actions last year, cheered along with you when Michael Gove finally got gone and the Chicago Teachers Union and its members have been following the Stand Up for Education Campaign and watching how parents and community have sympathized with teachers and their 60 hour work weeks.

I'm here with two simple messages to you. One, you are not alone. Two, there are ways to fight back and win. I had the pleasure of participating last spring in a wonderful conference hosted by the NUT where educators from all over the world came to discuss the Global Education Reform Movement, the GERM. We heard about the ways that public education is being destroyed by business interests in a calculated, coordinated way. The same types of initiatives I see in Chicago and across the United States are the exact same ones being used in Asia, Africa, South and Central America and of course here in the UK and in other parts of Europe. The attacks on our students and teachers take different forms in different places, with mutations to make the GERM more effective depending on where it is active. For example, in India, the GERM takes advantage of the caste system and all that encompasses. In Mexico, it uses corrupt police and government officials to disappear student teachers that stand up for public education. In the States, it attacks where communities are already weakened. New Orleans' entire school system was privatized immediately after Hurricane Katrina and the Secretary of Education, Arne Duncan, called it 'the best thing to happen to public education in New Orleans."Elsewhere budget crises prompt massive school closures, cuts to teachers' pensions and privatisation of public schools.

Looking at the *Stand Up for Education* pages on the NUT's website, I see many similarities between the GERM attacks on public education in the UK and back home. Your 'conversion"is our 'turnaround."Your 'appraisals"are our teacher and school rating systems, 'PERA" in my home state, which ties students' standardized test scores to teachers' performance ratings, and can lead to job loss. Your 'academies"are our 'charters," (they both mean privatisation). Some words are surrounded by controversy in both places.

Poverty: the real cause of alleged school failure. In Chicago and many other big cities, a student's postal zip code is the best predictor of standardised test performance.

Pensions: they want to take our hard earned retirement investments because bankers crashed the economy.

Testing: too much time on meaningless tests that don't measure anything but poverty levels (and they are used to make corporations rich).

Which leads me to Pearson. The Common Core State Standards imposed upon us by Pearson were created by non-educators, are woefully off-level, discourage critical thinking and the use of context. Imagine giving a student the Magna Carta to read, but leaving out all of the context! That is what the Common Core State Standards do! Workload is the number one complaint I hear from my members. They spend their days analysing data, restructuring their lesson plans, analysing data, reporting on the data, inserting five grades per class per week, analysing more data. Our special education teachers are so busy testing and doing paperwork that our kids don't receive their special education services.

BUT. There is hope. I'm here to let you know that teachers in the States are standing up and your own union is doing the same. The quick version of what happened in Chicago goes like this. Renaissance 2010 was devised as a plan to 'transform" the Chicago Public Schools. The plan was to close 100 'failing" schools and open 100 'successful" schools in their place. They targeted schools in poverty-stricken neighbourhoods, places with a lot of public housing, and where unemployment and gang violence were the norm. Instead of putting resources into the schools (which educators know would have been the real way to improve student learning), they closed them and replaced them with quasi-public/private charters. Tens of thousands of students were displaced, thousands of teachers and school support staff lost their jobs and what replaced them were novice, unqualified teachers who didn't know what they were doing, who were being led by people who weren't educators. And this was supposed to 'close the inequality gap!"You won't be surprised to hear it didn't work.

Neighbourhood schools are the centre of community. They hold things together, especially in neighbourhoods with nothing else. They started with five to ten schools being closed for performance, then ten to twenty for performance, under-utilization, bad test scores, whatever they could invent as criteria. This continued for a decade.

Early in 2008, a group of teachers had had enough. We started organizing to fight back. My school, along with 15 others was placed on the chopping block. Social justice minded teachers got together to see what could be done. We started with a book club reading *The Shock Doctrine* by Naomi Klein if you haven't read it, you should. What we realized was that we already had the mechanism to fight back, we just weren't utilising it correctly. Chicago teachers belong to the Chicago Teachers Union, Local 1 of the American Federation of Teachers. It was formed in the fight backs of the past, tracing its roots to the early 20th century.

We forced our union to look at its role and its potential power differently. We no longer wanted bread and butter or service unionism, we wanted members to become active, to control their own destiny. We wanted to see an end to reactive actions to things being done TO us we wanted to change the course.

Importantly, we also saw the need to bring in other stake holders. We were tired of the 'THEM"controlling our schools and our futures. We wanted to, saw the imperative to, band the 'Uses"together. There were more of US than THEM. We, the US, knew more about our students and communities than the THEM and we knew that to change anything, we'd need each other.

We formed a coalition which we named GEM—The Grassroots Education Movement. It included community groups, mostly from neighbourhoods of colour, those that had been targeted in closures. There were also parent groups, some that had been fighting virtually alone for years. There was a teacher group other than the union, a group of social justice-minded teachers that emphasized empowering students through their teaching methods and curricula. Coalition work is tough, and should be. If you are truly bringing together different representative groups, those groups will at times have competing notions, different motivations, different focuses and all those forces will pull in different directions. But if your overall goal is the same, and ours was, to protect and preserve public education in the city of Chicago, you can find ways to make it work.

The relationships, common language, friendships and solidarity that we fomented in that early coalition continue to this day. The roots of those coalitions helped the Chicago Teachers Union launch and win a successful week and a half long strike. Months before our strike, while we were organizing school building by school building, our coalition partners helped guide us in the creation of our research paper, "The Schools Chicago's Students Deserve." Based on the priorities of our teachers and parents and community members we worked with, we developed a road map, not unlike your Stand Up for Education Manifesto. We laid out our vision of what schooling should be fully staffed and resourced schools, arts, music, physical education for all students, wrap around services like nursing and social work for our students, especially those living in trauma. The solution to so-called failing schools wasn't to shutter them or fill them with unqualified teachers, it was to provide them with what they had been lacking for decades.

Through the report and the demands we made we won the public to our side. They saw that we weren't just fighting for teachers' salaries or pensions, but that the teachers were fighting for their children. In return, the parents and community fought for our teachers. Our message was simple—we wanted the same things for our students that the mayor's kids had. Since the message was so simple yet so broad, our members were great at articulating it. Any of our members were capable of pleading our case to parents and their neighbours with personal stories of what their schools and classrooms were lacking.

Teachers' strikes are rarely popular, but ours was. Teachers, parents and supporters rallied by their schools in the mornings, then marched downtown in the afternoons. They shut the business district down every day for 9 days. Remarkably, the support did not just come from Chicago. Teachers and unionists from across the country parachuted in to town to lend a hand. On the sixth day of our strike a poll showed that fully 60% of the parents in the city still supported us---an unheard of number!

We ended up winning a lot in our contract. Huge monetary gains for our members weren't one of those wins. But you know what? Our members didn't mind. We had won back some dignity, some pride, and some improved conditions for our students.

Most importantly, we built more lasting coalitions and found more allies. The CTU is now the trusted voice on education issues in the city of Chicago. Parents and the media alike turn to us for guidance. Since the strike we've had testing opt outs led by parents and teachers. Sadly, we've also been punished. The mayor closed 50 schools in a single year and is about to pay the political price for it. On Tuesday we'll hold the first mayoral run-off election in decades and our neoliberal mayor will hopefully be unseated by a low profile politician that represents working class people across the city. Even if the mayor somehow hangs on to his job, he's taken a hit that will hopefully hurt his presidential ambitions.

Excitingly, the movement has caught fire. Unions across the states have copied our plan and expanded it. There are now documents describing the schools St. Paul's, Los Angeles's, Seattle's, and Milwaukee's Students deserve. Each modified and expanded to meet their particular needs. Our fight back network continues to grow ad our tactics continue to evolve. It feels as though we are becoming the penicillin to the GERM. We are weakening it even though it is still fighting.

A critical, yet basic union principle tells me that we will win. There are more of us than them. We are growing faster and stronger than them. Each victorious strike, each well-written student-focused manifesto makes us stronger.

Thank you so much for having me. I cannot wait to see the fierce teachers of the National Union of Teachers take the baton and lead the next chapter of this battle.

I look forward to learning from you.

Solidarity forever!

1   This is the text of the solidarity speech given by Kristine to the 2015 NUT Annual Conference on behalf of the Chicago Teachers' Union.
2   Sadly, Rahm Emmanuel won a second term as mayor of Chicago. But a ray of hope is that Susan Sadlowski Garza, a school counsellor and CTU Area Vice President and school delegate, was elected to City Council. Sue and the other 12 members of the Progressive Caucus will continue the fight in the council and we are proud to have a union sister representing us there.

Notes